PROSPERITY EDUCATION

WORK IT OUT

with PHRASAL VERBS

TEACHING RESOURCE
B2–C1

BILLIE JAGO
MONICA RUDA-PEACHEY

PROSPERITY EDUCATION

Registered offices: Sherlock Close, Cambridge
CB3 0HP, United Kingdom

© Prosperity Education Ltd. 2020

First published 2020

ISBN: 978-1-9161297-2-6

This publication is in copyright. Subject to statutory exception
and to the provisions of relevant collective licensing agreements,
no reproduction of any part may take place without the written
permission of Prosperity Education.

The moral rights of the authors have been asserted.

Typeset and produced by ORP Cambridge

Cover design by Frill Creative www.frillcreative.com

For further information and resources, visit:
www.prosperityeducation.net

To infinity and beyond.

Contents

About this book	5
Introduction	6
Phrasal verb overview	7
Work out 1: Advice	9
Work out 2: Family	13
Work out 3: Holidays	17
Work out 4: Relationships	20
Work out 5: Eating and drinking	24
Work out 6: Dreams	27
Work out 7: Crime	31
Work out 8: Business	35
Work out 9: Shopping	39
Work out 10: Health	45
Worksheets	49
Extra practice	79
Phrasal verb reference	95
Download code	100

About this book

Work it Out with Phrasal verbs

Designed for both new and experienced teachers, *Work It Out with Phrasal Verbs* is uniquely focused on presenting and practising phrasal verbs in context, away from the common method of verb or particle grouping. With its highly communicative, student-centred approach, *Work It Out with Phrasal Verbs* offers downloadable and photocopiable lesson materials, extensive teaching notes and a variety of inclusive activities for B2–C1 level students.

Key features

- Detailed lesson plans to ensure clear and effective delivery, from start to finish, including lead-ins and activities for practice, production and extension
- Activities and lesson adaptations to accommodate the needs of mixed-ability classes, and discussion questions to encourage critical thinking
- Digital alternatives, online-teaching tips and a front-of-class presentation tool to support a blended-learning environment
- Extension exercises for more-confident students and activities for fast finishers

Downloadable and photocopiable content

- Front-of-class presentations
- Worksheets
- Extra practice activities
- Phrasal verb overview handout
- Phrasal verb dictionary

About the authors

Billie Jago is an ELT writer, consultant and teacher trainer who creates digital learning materials and assessment resources for National Geographic and Pearson Education. Having previously taught internationally, she now delivers online training seminars to global teaching audiences.

Monica Ruda-Peachey is an ELT writer who creates digital and print teaching resources and exam items. She is a DELTA-qualified ESL teacher and Trinity-certified teacher trainer with extensive experience teaching English to international students in the Czech Republic, Italy and the UK.

Introduction

Preparing to work it out

To make the most of the activities in this book and to maximize students' learning, we strongly recommend that you read this introductory section when using *Work it Out with Phrasal Verbs* for the first time. *The phrasal verb overview* (page 7) has been designed to summarise what a teacher needs to keep in mind when presenting phrasal verbs to their class. It has been written using uncomplicated language, should you decide to give it as a handout to your students.

Work it Out with Phrasal Verbs aims to support teachers in:

- presenting phrasal verbs in contexts that easily tie in with common coursebook topics
- delivering adaptable lessons depending on the specific needs of each class
- promoting classroom inclusion.

As classes come in all abilities and sizes, each unit offers a number of features:

- digital alternatives, tips and a front-of-class presentation tool
- extension activities
- alternative activities
- adaptations for less-confident students
- activities for fast finishers
- expected timings for each activity
- worksheets and answer keys

Each of the ten units is called a *Work out* and these can be worked through sequentially or used as standalone lessons. If standalone, we recommend the following preparatory steps:

1. Write an example sentence on the board using one of the phrasal verbs from the lesson you intend to teach.
2. Have pupils identify the phrasal verb.
3. Elicit what a phrasal verb is by asking questions.

To help you to introduce phrasal verbs for the first time, you can use *the phrasal verb overview* (page 7) and *the phrasal verb reference* (pages 95–99).

We hope this resource proves a useful companion to you when working out phrasal verbs with your students.

Billie Jago and Monica Ruda-Peachey
Cambridge, 2020

Phrasal verb overview

What you need to know about phrasal verbs

- Phrasal verbs are composed of two parts: a verb and a particle – e.g. *look after*.
- Keeping the same verb but changing the particle will affect the whole meaning of the phrasal verb – e.g. *look after/look for/look into*.
- Phrasal verbs are part of informal, everyday language. Their synonym is usually more formal, and it often has Latin or Greek origins – e.g. *carry on = continue*.
- Phrasal verbs can be *inseparable* (intransitive) or *separable* (transitive).

Inseparable (intransitive) phrasal verbs always follow this pattern, which cannot be changed:

Subject (S)	Verb (V)	Particle (P)	Object (O)
Sara	grew	up	in Spain

Separable (transitive) phrasal verbs can follow two different patterns:

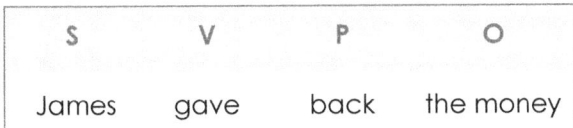

Or:

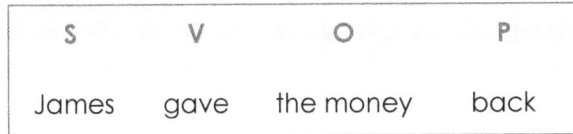

Notice how the object and the particle have swapped places.

Be careful! If the object (the money) is replaced by a pronoun (it), only **one** pattern is correct:

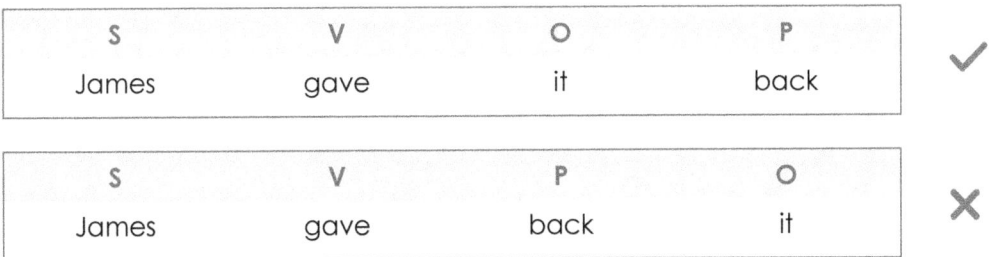

Work out 1

Advice

'When nothing goes right… go left.'

B2

Resources	Worksheet 1.1	one copy per group
	Worksheet 1.2	one copy per group
	Worksheet 1.3	one copy per student
	Worksheet 1.4	one copy per student

Target language

Ask around – to speak to many people to find the answer

Calm down – to become, or make somebody become, less excited, anxious or upset

Check out – to take a look at something

Cheer up – to make yourself, or someone else, feel happier

Keep on – to maintain doing something

Look into (something) – to do research to find something

Set on (doing something) – to be sure you are going to achieve a planned objective

Speak up – to express opinions freely and honestly

Take on – to begin, or take responsibility for, something

Think over – to reflect on something

1

o Put students into groups. Write the following questions on the board:

Who do you usually ask for advice? Are you good at giving advice? Why/Why not?

5–10 mins

o Get students' feedback. Encourage them to share their reasons for 'Why?'/'Why not?'.

o Ask students what they think an 'Agony Aunt' is (a magazine or newspaper column that offers suggestions to readers who have requested help for a specific problem – usually love, friendship or family-related).

> **Digital tip**
> Ask students to search online for the meaning of 'Agony Aunt' and find what the most common topics are.

Work it Out with Phrasal Verbs Work out 1: Advice

2
- Give each group **Worksheet 1.1**. Students read the problems and discuss possible solutions.

5–10 mins

- Students share ideas as a class and vote for the best solution for each problem.

- Give each group **Worksheet 1.2**. Have students match each problem with the right response.

- Check answers as a whole class.

Answer key	
Worksheets 1.1 and 1.2	Julia: C Aida: A Jack: B

Extension
Have groups discuss what advice they would give for each problem. Encourage students to give their reasons why.

3
- Put students into pairs and give them a copy of **Worksheet 1.3**.

15–20 mins

- Have students match the definitions to the phrasal verbs.

- Get students' feedback and provide further examples or explanations if necessary.

Answer key	
Worksheet 1.3	1 C; 2 F; 3 D; 4 G; 5 A; 6 E; 7 I; 8 B; 9 J; 10 H

Fast finishers
Using Worksheet 1.3, have pairs write three sentences that each include at least one phrasal verb, to check for understanding.

- Explain that the phrasal verbs in Worksheet 1.3 can be used to replace some phrases in the problems (Worksheet 1.1) and responses (Worksheet 1.2).

- Give each student a copy of **Worksheet 1.4** and ask them to find the phrasal verb *calm down*. Tell them to look at the first line in Response B (Worksheet 1.2). Explain that *take a deep breath and relax* can be replaced by *calm down*.

Work it Out with Phrasal Verbs   Work out 1: Advice

- Put students into pairs. Have them look for phrases in worksheets 1.1 and 1.2 that can be replaced by the phrasal verbs in Worksheet 1.4. Explain that they only appear once – either in the problems or the responses: they cannot appear in both.

- Encourage students to refer to Worksheet 1.3 if they need help with definitions.

- Get students' feedback.

Answer key Worksheet 1.4	1. check out – Problem, Jack: 'to have a look at' 2. speak up – Response C: 'say anything' 3. keep on – Problem, Aida: 'continue' 4. take on – Problem, Aida: 'doing' 5. calm down – Response B: 'take a deep breath and relax' 6. think over – Response C: 'reflect on what they've done' (full answer: 'think over/think it over') 7. cheer up – Response B: 'be happy' 8. set on (doing something) – Problem, Aida: 'determined to' 9. look into – Response B: 'take a look at' 10. ask around – Response A: 'speak to people'

Alternative activity
Draw the table on the board and give a marker to each pair. Have students come and write their answers.

4

- In pairs, students think of a problem. Give your own example if necessary (e.g. *I crashed my sister's car; someone is stealing from work; etc.*).

25–30 mins

- Have each pair write a problem, using Worksheet 1.1 to help them. Remind students to include some of the phrasal verbs from the lesson. Monitor and assist as necessary.

- Once completed, have pairs pass their problem to the pair on their left. Have them think of a reponse (solution) and write it underneath.

- Continue this way until each pair has written a response to each problem. For larger classes, continue until four or five pairs have written a response.

- Once the problem is returned to the original pair, have pairs read the problem and the responses received to the class.

- Note down any errors to write on the board. Elicit corrections from the class.

Work out 2

Family

'Treat your family like friends and your friends like family.'

B2

| Resources | Worksheet 2.1 | one copy per group |
| | Teaching tool 2.1 | one teacher copy |

Target language

Bring up – to take care of someone until they are an adult

Fall out (with) – to argue with someone and to no longer have a relationship

Get on/along (with) – to have a good relationship with someone

Grow up – the process by which you went from being a child to an adult

Look after – to take care of someone/something

Look like – to look similar to another person

Look up to – to admire someone

Split up – to end a relationship (e.g. a couple separating, often divorcing)

Tell off – to reprimand/scold someone

1
- Tell the class the following story. Use your own ideas or invent them if preferred.

    I grew up in _____, which is in _____.

    I was brought up by _____ in a _____.

    I have _____ brothers/sisters who I get on very well with.

- Put students into pairs and have them discuss their house type, the area they are from and if they have any brothers or sisters.

- Give prompts on the board if necessary.

5–10 mins

2
- Put students into small groups and give each pair or group a board pen. Explain that they are going to have a quiz, and that groups will be awarded points for correct answers.

- Divide the board into columns: one column for each group of students (e.g. If there are five groups, draw five columns on the board).

5–10 mins

Work it Out with Phrasal Verbs   Work out 2: Family

- ○ Give a copy of **Worksheet 2.1** to each group. Ask students to read the phrasal verbs and discuss whether they know the meanings of any. Do not elicit any ideas at this stage.

> **Alternative activity**
> If mini whiteboards are available, have students write their answers on them and show their answers when ready. Award points for correct answers.

3

- ○ Explain that you are going to read, or project, if possible, sentences with the phrasal verbs missing. Use **PT 2.1**. Tell students to discuss the options and decide on their answer. Explain that they will have ten seconds to decide, then should come and write their answers on the board.

15–20 mins

PT 2.1

- ○ Read, or display, the sentences in **Teaching tool 2.1** to the students. If projecting, reveal the sentences one by one. Countdown from 10 or show a visible timer to the class.

- ○ When time is up, have one student per group come to the board and write their answer in their column. Repeat the steps.

- ○ Get students' feedback. Encourage them to explain the definitions.

> **Teaching tool 2.1**
>
> 1. My sister was very naughty when she was younger. My mum used to _____ all the time!
>
> 2. People always tell me I _____ my mum because we both have very blonde hair.
>
> 3. My dad hasn't lived with me for about ten years; my parents _____ when I was very young.
>
> 4. I really _____ my grandma; she's very inspirational, and I hope I can be just like her when I'm older.
>
> 5. My mum has always worked very hard, so when I was younger my grandparents used to _____ me a lot of the time when Mum was at work.
>
> 6. My cousin and I _____ because he started dating my ex-girlfriend!
>
> 7. My sister is _____ her children really well; they're very polite and kind children, and not selfish at all.
>
> 8. My sister-in-law is so lovely, we _____ very well and have a lot in common; we spend a lot of time together.
>
> 9. I _____ on a farm in the countryside, so I'm used to spending a lot of time outdoors and around animals.

Work it Out with Phrasal Verbs   Work out 2: Family

Answer key	
Worksheet 2.1	1 C; 2 A; 3 B; 4 C; 5 C; 6 A; 7 A; 8 B; 9 C

4
- Write the following on the board: *Did you _____ in the city or the countryside?*
- Ask the class which phrasal verb they would use to complete the question (*grow up*).
- Ask students to individually write five questions to ask someone about their family. Encourage them to use the target language. For example:

Who do you look up to in your family? Why? Who do you get on with in class or at home?

10–15 mins

Fast finishers
Encourage students to write extra questions to ask their classmates.

5
- Have students walk around the class and ask their questions to three or four other students.
- Explain that students should choose one of the students they spoke to and share the information about their chosen classmate to the rest of the class. Have students guess who it could be.

15–20 mins

Alternative activity
Have students write three sentences about their chosen classmate on a piece of paper. Tell them to keep it a secret. Ask students to screw up their paper, then stand up and throw it in the air. Have students pick up a random piece of paper and read its content aloud, for the class to guess who it describes.

6
- Explain that students are going to give a presentation about their families to the class. Tell them they can use a famous or fictional family if they prefer. They must use at least five of the phrasal verbs from the target language. Students can work individually, or in pairs.
- Encourage them to use pictures or illustrations, and to provide extra information about their family (e.g. personality adjectives, hobbies, etc.).

30–40 mins

- Give students prompts if necessary:

    Where did you grow up? Who with?

    Do you look like anyone in your family?

    Who do you look up to? Why?

    Who have you always got on with in your family?

- Have students share their presentations with the class. Encourage questions from the audience after each presentation, to find out further information. For less-confident students, have students present in small groups.

Digital tip

Have students make their presentations on a digital presentation platform, either at home or in class. Encourage students to personalise their slides using photos of their hometown, who they look like, etc.

Work out 3

Holidays

'It's better to see something once than to hear about it a hundred times.'

B2

Resources	Worksheet 3.1	one copy per student
	Worksheet 3.2	one copy per student in Team A
	Worksheet 3.3	one copy per student in Team B

Target language

Check in – to confirm that you have arrived at a hotel or airport

Check out – to leave a hotel after returning your room key

Eat out – to have a meal in a restaurant, not at home

Get in/into – to enter a place

Go away – to leave a place (often to spend time somewhere else, usually on holiday)

Take (some time) off – to have a break from work for a few days

Take off – to begin to fly (e.g. an aeroplane or helicopter)

Wait around – to wait somewhere for something

1

o Write the following questions on the board:

When was the last time you went away on holiday?

Do you often take time off from working or studying?

What is your favourite part of flying? Why?

o Put students into pairs to discuss the questions. Invite pairs to share their ideas with the class.

5–10 mins

2

o Hand out one copy of **Worksheet 3.1** to each student.

o Have students match A–H with 1–8.

o Have students compare their answers in pairs, then ask them to underline the phrasal verb in each sentence. Ask them to discuss what they think each phrasal verb means.

o Get feedback. Discuss any definitions and go through pronunciation as necessary.

10–15 mins

Answer key	
Worksheet 3.1	A 5 B 8 C 1 D 7 E 2 F 4 G 6 H 3

> **Alternative activity**
>
> Ask more-confident students to think of a synonym, or a phrase with a similar meaning, for each phrasal verb in Worksheet 3.1. Get feedback. Have the class choose the best synonyms to compile their own Phrasal Verb Dictionary in their notebooks.
>
> Have students use the synonym or alternative phrase to rewrite the sentences in Worksheet 3.1.

3
- Divide the class into Team A and Team B. Give **Worksheet 3.2** to Team A and **Worksheet 3.3** to Team B.
- Tell students to interview as many classmates from the opposite team as possible. Explain that they should ask only one question per student.
- Ask students to note down the name and answer of the students they interview.

15–20 mins

4
- Organise students into groups of three or four. Explain that individuals within the groups can be awarded points during the activity. The student with most points in each group at the end is the winner.
- In groups, students share the information gathered during the interview. Encourage them to use full sentences, including the relevant phrasal verb and the name of the student they interviewed.
- Explain that one point is awarded for including the name of the student, and two points are awarded for including a relevant phrasal verb in the sentence. Give examples if needed:

  Davide goes away on holiday once a year. ('Davide' – 1 point; 'goes away' – 2 points)

- After each student shares their piece of information, the groups decide whether the sentence produced is satisfactory in order to achieve one, two or three points.
- Have the winner of each group share some of their sentences with the class.

20–25 mins

Work it Out with Phrasal Verbs   Work out 3: Holidays

Digital tip

Using a free quiz app maker (e.g. Kahoot!), use phrasal verbs and their definitions to create a quiz. For example:

To inform that you have arrived at a hotel to receive the keys for your room.

A. *Check in*   B. *Wait around*   C. *Get in*   D. *Check out*

To have a break from work for a few days.

A. *Take time out*   B. *Take time off*   C. *Check out*   D. *Go away*

To have a meal in a restaurant, not at home.

A. *Go away*   B. *Eat in*   C. *Take away*   D. *Eat out*

Fast finishers

Have students write three sentences about their findings (e.g. *When Khalid eats out, he likes to eat pizza because he says it tastes better in a restaurant than at home*).

Encourage students to include any phrasal verbs from the lesson.

Extension

Have students write about one of their holidays, using as many phrasal verbs from the lesson as possible. This can be done in class or assigned as homework.

Work out 4

Relationships

'I'm only saving your number so I'll know not to answer when you call.'

B2+

Resources	Worksheet 4.1	one copy per student in Group A
	Worksheet 4.2	one copy per student in Group B
	Worksheet 4.3	one copy per pair
	Worksheet 4.4	one copy per pair

Target language

Ask out – to invite someone to go out with you

Break up/split up – to end a relationship

Fall for – to begin to love someone

Get on with – to have a good relationship with someone

Hit it off – to have an instant connection with someone

Lead on – to make someone think you are interested in them, even though you are not

Make up – to become friends after having an argument

Settle down – to start a family and have children

Stand up – if someone arranges to meet you and they don't come

Turn down – to say 'no' to an invitation to go out

1

- Write the following on the board (or use **PT 4.1**):

    Who do you have a good relationship with in your family?

    Have you ever had an instant connection with someone you have just met?

    By what age would you like to have a stable job and your own family?

- Put students into pairs to discuss the questions. Ask one or two pairs to share their ideas with the class.

- Explain that there are other ways to ask these questions using phrasal verbs. Write the following on the board (or use PT 4.1):

    Settle down   Hit it off   Get on with

- In pairs, have students decide which part of each question can be replaced by the phrasal verbs. Get feedback.

10–15 mins

PT 4.1

Answer key Presentation 4.1	1. Who do you ~~have a good relationship with~~ **get on with** in your family?
	2. Have you ever ~~had an instant connection~~ **hit it off** with someone you've just met?
	3. By what age would you like to ~~have a stable job and your own family~~ **settle down**?

2

20–25 mins

- Divide the class into two groups and give one copy of **Worksheet 4.1** to each student in Group A, and one copy of **Worksheet 4.2** to each student in Group B. Cut the worksheets into strips, as marked, and reorder them.

- Explain that each group has a different story. Tell students to put the sections in order to create the stages of the relationship in each story.

- Have students underline the phrasal verbs in the story.

- In the same groups, ask students to think of a synonym to replace the phrasal verb. Do the first as a class, as an example (e.g. *ask out* – invite someone on a date).

- Ask students to write a simple definition for each of the phrasal verbs in the story.

Answer key Worksheet 4.1	D; A; C; B; E

Answer key Worksheet 4.2	C; E; D; A; B

3

15–20 mins

- Explain that groups are going to teach the other group the phrasal verbs in their story and the definitions they have written.

- Have members of Group A each read one part of their story aloud and ask Group B to consider what the meaning and definition is after each turn. Have them say this out loud.

- Encourage every student in Group A to read. Once Group B has guessed, have students in Group A correct them if necessary.

- Switch roles.

Alternative activity

Have groups take it in turns to write the verbs from their story on one side of the board and the prepositions on the other. Ask the other group to match them and to discuss what they think the meaning is, before reading the story aloud to check.

Extension

Put students into pairs and give each pair a copy of **Worksheet 4.3**. Have students read the clues and write the correct phrasal verb into the correct space in the crossword.

Answer key	1 – make up
Worksheet 4.3	2 – lead on
	3 – fall for
	4 – ask out
	5 – get on with
	6 – stand up
	7 – hit it off
	8 – break up
	9 – settle down
	10 – turn down

4

- Give each student a copy of **Worksheet 4.4**. Invite a student to read the first sentence aloud.

- Ask: *How can we make this a question? What tense do we need to use?*

- Elicit ideas and write the answer on the board (Have you ever been asked out?; present perfect).

- For lower-level classes, turn each sentence into a question as a class and write them on the board. For higher-level classes, allow time for students to do this individually.

- Have students walk around the room and ask their classmates the questions. Encourage them to make notes of the students' names and what they say.

10–15 mins

Digital alternative

Encourage students to set up online calls with two or three of their classmates to discuss their ideas. Organise the groups in advance and have students agree on a time for their call.

5

- Give each student a piece of paper. Explain that they are going to create their own story about relationships, using phrasal verbs from the lesson. Explain that there will be two characters who meet for the first time.

25–30 mins

- Write the following on the board:

Famous man

- Have students write the name of a famous man at the top of their piece of paper. Explain that they can be a writer, singer, actor, sportsperson, or whoever they can think of.

- Have students fold the top of the paper, so that the name is covered, and pass it to the person on their left. Tell students not to look at what their classmate has written.

- Write on the board:

Famous woman

- Repeat the steps. Fold the paper and pass it to the left.

- In stages, write the following on the board:

A place (e.g. the kitchen, a restaurant, on the Moon)

The first date (e.g. he asked her out; they hit it off straight away)

How the friendship progressed (e.g. they fell for each other; XX asked out XX but XX turned them down; etc.)

What happened at the end of the story (e.g. he wanted to settle down; she broke up with him; etc.)

- Explain that students can be as funny and imaginative as they wish. Encourage them to use phrasal verbs in their stories. Have students fold and pass their pieces of paper after writing each stage.

- After the final stage, have students open their pieces of paper. Give students time to read their stories.

- In pairs or small groups, students share their stories with each other. Monitor and take notes for delayed error correction.

- Invite one or two students to share their stories with the class.

Work out 5

Eating and drinking

'Life is like a sandwich: you have to fill it with the best ingredients.'

B2

Resources	Worksheet 5.1	one copy per student in Group A
	Worksheet 5.2	one copy per student in Group B
	Worksheet 5.3	one copy per student

Target language

Cut out – to eliminate something from your diet

Eat in – to have a meal at home (not in a restaurant)

Eat out – to have a meal at a restaurant (not at home)

Fill yourself up – to eat so much that you are no longer hungry

Go off – when the food has passed its expiry date and can no longer be eaten

Pick at – to have many small snacks instead of a full meal

Put on (weight) – becoming bigger and heavier

Serve up – to put food onto plates, ready to be eaten

Slice up – to cut food into pieces to be shared (e.g. a pizza)

Take away – to order food from a restaurant but to eat it at home

Top up (the glass) – to add more drink when there isn't much left

Wash down (with) – to have a drink during a meal

Wolf down – to eat very quickly and in a large quantity

1

- In small groups, students discuss the following questions:

  Can you keep in shape and healthy without following any advice?

  What health advice do you know of? Do you follow any?

- Give your own examples if necessary (e.g. Eat five portions of fruit or vegetables a day). After the discussion, students share their ideas with the class.

5–10 mins

> **Digital tip**
>
> Give the questions to students before the online lesson for them to note down any ideas. Provide feedback in the lesson. If your video platform allows it, use the 'breakout rooms' to organise students into groups.

2

o Divide the class into two groups, and give one copy of **Worksheet 5.1** to each student in Group A, and one copy of **Worksheet 5.2** to each student in Group B.

5–10 mins

o Groups discuss the following questions (write them on the board if necessary):

What is the purpose of this text? Who might be interested in reading this text?

o Get students' feedback.

| Answer key
Worksheet
5.1: Group A | 1. To give advice on how to avoid gaining weight and to keep healthy.
2. Anyone who is concerned about their weight and health. |

| Answer key
Worksheet
5.2: Group B | 1. To give advice on how to enjoy your food while keeping healthy.
2. Anyone who enjoys eating with friends. |

3

o In the same groups, students look at the phrasal verbs (worksheets 5.1 and 5.2) and discuss their meaning. Explain that they do not need to write at this stage.

5–10 mins

o Monitor both groups to provide help and guidance on definitions if needed.

> Alternative activity
>
> Have students infer the meaning of the phrasal verbs individually, then compare their definitions to an online dictionary.

4

o Have students write their own sentences using the phrasal verbs from the text (worksheets 5.1 and 5.2).

15–20 mins

o Put each student from Group A with a student from Group B to make pairs. Ask students to read their sentences to their partners for them to identify the phrasal verb and guess the meaning from context.

o Monitor pairs and provide support if necessary.

> Fast finishers
>
> Ask pairs to look at Worksheet 5.1 and discuss whether they agree or disagree with the dos and don'ts listed. Encourage them to give reasons why.

5

- Individually, students complete **Worksheet 5.3**. Tell them they can only use each phrasal verb once. Students then compare their answers in pairs.

5–10 mins

- Get feedback.

Answer key	1. pick at	5. cut out	10. gone off
Worksheet 5.3	2. top up	6. eat in	11. serves up
	3. wolf down	7. wash down	12. put on
	4. sliced up	8. take away	13. fill up
		9. eat out	

6

- As a class, brainstorm some locations in which people might eat and write these on the board (e.g. *a fast food restaurant, a Michelin-starred restaurant, grandmother's house, a picnic, etc.*). Put students into pairs and allocate a location to each pair.

25–30 mins

- Ask students to choose five phrasal verbs from the lesson. For less-confident students, have them choose fewer phrasal verbs.

- In their pairs, students discuss and write their own dos and don'ts of eating in their location, including their chosen phrasal verbs. Give your own examples if necessary (e.g. *The portions at a Michelin-starred restaurant won't fill me up; If I can't finish my food at a fast food restaurant, I can take it away; My grandmother's food is so good that I wolf it down in seconds!; I love picnics because I can pick at a lot of different food*).

- Encourage students to use their imaginations and put their ideas into a poster, infographic or presentation to share with the class.

> Digital alternative
>
> Have students make their presentation on a digital presentation platform to share with the class.

> Extension
>
> Students vote for which presentation should be awarded in various categories (e.g. *Best Design, Funniest Sentences, Best Phrasal Verb User, Best Presenter, etc.*). Encourage them to give a reason for their choice (e.g. *I'd like to award XX's presentation with Best Design because her pictures are unusual; XX deserves the Best Presenter award because he speaks very confidently*).
>
> Explain that students can't vote for their own presentation.

Work out 6

Dreams

'Keep the dream alive by not pressing the snooze button.'

B2+

Resources	Worksheet 6.1	one copy per student
	Worksheet 6.2	one strip per student
	Worksheet 6.3	one dream per pair
	Teaching tool 6.1	one teacher copy

Target language

Catch up – to share updates on each other's lives

Figure out – to understand something or to solve a problem

Go over (something) – to read something in detail

Hand over (something) – to pass an object to someone

Peel (something) off – to remove something that is tight or attached to something else

Pop over – to visit someone for a short period of time

Sign up for – to join a course or an activity

Sleep over – to spend the night at somebody else's house

Work out – to do exercise

1

o Tell students about a strange dream you've had (or use **PT 6.1**). Use the following example if preferred:

You're about to give a speech in front of an audience when you notice you are wearing pyjamas.

o Ask students what they think the dream means and elicit ideas.

o Ask: *Have you ever had unusual dreams?*

o Put students into pairs to discuss their ideas.

o Give prompts if necessary (e.g. going to school with everyone looking at you, winning money, falling, etc.).

o Invite students to share their dreams with the class.

o Encourage others to suggest what they think their classmates' dreams might mean.

5–10 mins

PT 6.1

2

- Write the following questions on the board (or use **PT 6.2**):

  1. *Where was I last Saturday afternoon and why did I go there?*
  2. *Where did I sleep? How did I sleep?*
  3. *What are the key points of my dream?*

- Explain that you're going to tell the class about one of your dreams. Tell students to listen out for the answers to the questions and to note these down.

- Read (or display) **Teaching tool 6.1** to the class, twice if necessary.

- Ask students to discuss their answers in pairs. Get feedback. Ask the class what they think the dream might mean.

10–15 mins

PT 6.2

Teaching tool 6.1

So, last Saturday afternoon **I popped over** *to my friend's house for a coffee and a chat. We hadn't seen each other in a long time so we wanted to catch up on each other's news. We decided to have dinner together so my friend* **rustled up** *a lovely meal. It was getting late so I agreed to* **sleep over** *at my friend's house. Even though the bed was nice and comfy, I had the weirdest dream! It started with me* **signing up** *for aerobics classes at a gym, where I could see lots of people* **working out**. *As I was* **going over** *the terms and conditions of my gym subscription, the receptionist patiently waited for me to* **hand over** *my debit card to pay. You can imagine my surprise when I realised that my debit card was stuck to my hand – I tried to* **peel it off** *but nothing! My hand just wouldn't let go of it!!! Can you* **figure out** *the meaning of this dream??*

Answer key 1 Teaching tool 6.1	1. I went to my friend's house for a coffee and a chat.
	2. I slept at my friend's house in a comfy bed, but I had a weird dream.
	3. Joining a gym; people doing exercise; reading a contract carefully; debit card stuck to my hand/I couldn't pay.

3

- Tell students that they are going to listen to the dream again. Put students in A and B pairs.

- Have Student A prepare to take notes of the phrasal verbs they will hear. Tell Student B to take notes of the nouns that are related to the phrasal verbs.

- Do the first as a class, as an example (e.g. *pop over – my friend's house*).

- Read Teaching tool 6.1 to the class again, twice if necessary. Have students take notes.

15–20 mins

- Tell pairs to match their phrasal verbs and nouns.
- Get feedback. Write students' answers on the board.
- Ask students to think of other nouns that could replace those on the board and discuss them in pairs. Give suggestions if necessary (e.g. going over an important document; popping over to your parent's house).
- Get feedback. Add students' ideas to the board.
- Encourage students to make notes.

Answer key 2 Teaching tool 6.1	popped over – to my friend's house
	rustled up – a lovely meal
	sleep over – at my friend's house
	signing up – for aerobics classes/at the gym
	working out – people/at the gym
	going over – the terms and conditions/gym subscription
	hand over – my debit card
	peel off – my debit card/from my hand
	figure out – the meaning/the dream

Extension
In small groups, students use the new combinations of phrasal verbs and nouns presented on the board to write a short story. This can also be assigned as homework.

4
- Before the lesson, cut up strips from **Worksheet 6.2**.
- Give one copy of **Worksheet 6.1** to each student.

10–15 mins

- Use tape to stick the strips from Worksheet 6.2 onto the back of each student. If you have more than ten students, the same strips can be used for more than one person.
- Tell students to walk around the class and discuss the definitions attached to their classmates' backs, matching each to Worksheet 6.1. Have students write the name of the person that has each definition.
- Nominate individual students to share the definitions and who they found them on with the rest of the class.

Work it Out with Phrasal Verbs — Work out 6: Dreams

| Answer key Worksheets 6.1 and 6.2 | 1 G; 2 J; 3 D; 4 D; 5 I; 6 C; 7 A; 8 E; 9 F; 10 H |

5
- Put students into pairs and give each pair a different dream from **Worksheet 6.3**.
- Ask them to discuss their dream and decide its meaning. Encourage them to try and use some of the phrasal verbs. Tell them that they have four minutes. Set a visible timer.
- When time is up, have each pair pass their dream to the pair on their left. Then, have pairs discuss a new meaning to the new dream.
- Students continue to pass the dreams until each pair has discussed the meanings of all the dreams.
- Invite pairs to share some of their ideas with the class.

Dep. on numbers

> **Digital alternative**
>
> Ask students to search online for a dream and its meaning. Provide search terms if necessary (e.g. meanings of dreams; strange dream meanings; etc.).
>
> Have students make notes of the dream. Encourage them to try to use phrasal verbs from the lesson.
>
> Put students into pairs. Have one student tell their partner the dream and have them guess the meaning. Switch roles.
>
> Invite students to share their dreams with the class.

Work out 7

Crime

'Just remember: if we get caught, we don't speak English.'

B2/C1

Resources		
	Worksheet 7.1	one copy per student
	Worksheet 7.2	Story A – one copy for Group A
	Worksheet 7.2	Story B – one copy for Group B
	Worksheet 7.3	one copy per judge, with as many copies as there are rounds

Target language

Blow up – to create an explosion

Break in – to enter a building that is not yours

Get away with – to avoid punishment for a crime you have committed

Knock (someone) out – to fight with someone until they lose consciousness

Let (someone) off – to not punish someone for their crime or bad actions

Lock up – when someone is put in prison

Pull (someone) over – when the police signal for your car to move to the side of the road

Stake out – to sit outside a place to observe what is happening

Turn (someone) in – to tell the authorities of someone who has committed a crime

---

1
- In small groups, ask students to brainstorm any crimes they know (e.g. pickpocketing, theft, vandalism, etc.).

5–10 mins

- Give a board marker to each group. In turn, one student from each group writes their crimes on the board. Teacher discretion is advised as to what crimes are written on the board.

- Go through definitions where necessary.

2
- Write the following headlines on the board:

  Panic Package!; Motorway Fight; Finally Found; The most criminal place in the city

10–15 mins

- Explain that these are some crimes that have happened around the world.

Work it Out with Phrasal Verbs   Work out 7: Crime

- o In small groups, ask students to discuss what the crime for each headline may be. Invite groups to share their ideas.

- o Give each student a copy of **Worksheet 7.1** and have them read the texts. Have students say whether their predictions were correct.

- o Ask students to read the stories again and to underline the phrasal verbs that they find. Encourage them to help each other.

- o Have students share the phrasal verbs they found. Check the infinitive form of the phrasal verbs.

Answer key Worksheet 7.1	A. Panic Package!: break in; blew up (*blow up*); had broken out (*break out*) B. Motorway Fight: pulled (the driver) over (*pull over*); knocked out (*knock out*) C. Finally Found: turned (himself) in (*turn in*); get away with D. The Most Criminal Place in the City: staking out (*stake out*); locked up (*lock up*); let off

3

- o Put students into small groups. Cut up **Worksheet 7.2** – Story A and Story B – into strips, reorder them and give a copy to each group.

5–10 mins

- o Have students put the strips in order to recreate the story.

- o Encourage students to read their stories to the class.

Answer key Worksheet 7.2	Story A 2 6 3 1 5 4	Story B 3 1 4 6 5 2

Alternative activity
Set the task as a timed, competitive activity. Turn the pieces of paper over, start a timer and have groups compete to put their story in the correct order first.

Fast finishers
Write the following questions on the board. Have students discuss them in pairs.
Story A: *Do you think a 180-day sentence in prison is enough? Why/why not?* *Do you think the man was justified in robbing the bank? Why/why not?*	Story B: *Do you think the woman was justified in telling the police about John? Why/why not?* *Would you consider helping the police catch a criminal? Why/why not?*

4

- Tell students to read the story and find phrases that can be replaced with the phrasal verbs from Worksheet 7.1.

5–10 mins

- Do the first as a class as an example. Ask students to say which phrasal verb matches *fight them until they were unconscious* (knock them out).

- Get feedback.

Answer key Worksheet 7.2	Story A: 3. to fight them until they were unconscious! – *to knock them out* 1. escaped – *got away* 5. to move to the side of the road – *to pull over* 4. was put into prison – *was locked up* Story B: 3. to tell the police about John – *to turn John in* 1. to escape from prison – *to break out of prison* 4. to create an explosion – *to blow something up* 2. sitting outside John's house – *staking John out*

Digital alternative

Ask students to research an unusual crime that has recently happened in their country and to take note of the main points of the story. Remind them to include phrasal verbs from the lesson where possible. This task can be set as homework.

Ask students to retell the story to a partner or share it with the rest of the class.

5

- Write the following statement on the board:

  The victim of the crime should choose how long the offender is locked up for.

25–30 mins

- Ask the class to say whether they agree or disagree, and why.

- Divide the class into two groups. Explain that they're going to have a debate. Invite two students to be the judges, sitting at the front of the class.

- Write a debate topic on the board (e.g. *The punishment for the crime depends on the age of the suspect*).

- Allocate one team as 'for' and the other half as 'against'. Allow time for students to prepare some arguments for their given point of view.

- At the same time, have the judges work together to predict possible ideas that could be used in each debate. The role of the judges is to listen to the way in which each team expresses their opinion. Have the judges evaluate the arguments given, the range of vocabulary, and how many people in each team speak. Give the judges scorecards (**Worksheet 7.3**).

- Once the first round is over, write the next topic on the board and have the teams make notes of their ideas.

- Have the judges discuss the winning team in the first round. Encourage them to give praise to each team before announcing the winner.

- Repeat the steps. Give new copies of Worksheet 7.3 to the judges.

- Suggested debate topics:

    'If your friend commits a crime, you should always turn them in'.

    'If someone breaks out of prison, they should be allowed to remain free'.

    'When a serious crime is committed, the criminal should be locked up forever'.

    'If a crime is not serious, the suspect should be let off without any consequences'.

Work out 8

Business

'If Plan A fails, remember: you have 25 letters left.'

C1

| Resources | Worksheet 8.1 | one copy per student |
| | Worksheet 8.2 | one copy per pair |

Target language

Snowed under – to have a lot of work to do

Call in (sick) – to inform your workplace that you are too sick to work

Call off – to stop something from happening, such as a wedding or a meeting

Carry out – to perform or complete a task

Come up with – to think of something, such as an idea or a plan

Cut down – to decrease the quantity of something used

Get ahead – to be successful in one's job

Go ahead with – to start doing something after waiting for someone's permission

Note down – to write something down to avoid forgetting it

Rip off – to cheat someone by charging them too much money for something

Run by – to share your ideas with someone to hear their opinion

Run out – when something comes to an end, such as a contract or an agreement

Sell off – to sell something at a lower price because you need the money

Sign up – to subscribe or to join a group or a course

Stay behind – to not leave a place (school/work) when other people leave

Take on – to employ someone

Take over – to replace someone in their role

1
- Write the following question on the board:

    Which business do you consider successful? Why?

- Put students into small groups to discuss the question. Give your own example if necessary.

- Have groups share their ideas with the class. Encourage students to say whether or not they agree and why.

10–15 mins

Work it Out with Phrasal Verbs   Work out 8: Business

- Ask students: *What can a business do to reduce its expenses and increase profits?* Elicit ideas. Give your own idea to prompt students if necessary (e.g. Find less expensive ways of marketing, fewer staff, etc.).

- Get feedback.

2

- Give one copy of **Worksheet 8.1** to each student. Ask students to scan the text to get the general idea of it. Then ask the class:

5–10 mins

  What business is mentioned in the text? (a private language school)

  What is the problem? (students have complained; the number of students is declining)

  What are they doing to solve the problem? (carrying out a survey)

- Have students read the text again and answer questions 1–4.

- Have students check their answers in pairs. Get feedback.

Answer key Worksheet 8.1	1. It is a private language school that is having problems and receiving complaints.
	2. He is ambitious and wanted to improve the school when he first started, so made changes that were not agreed with his boss.
	3. Reduce the price of new courses; teachers need to work longer to design new courses; use less stationery; conduct a survey to find out the satisfaction rate within the school.
	4. Existing students are unhappy; a decrease in new students enrolling onto the courses; teachers are overworked; a high turnover of staff; lack of funds to invest in marketing campaigns.

Extension

Write the following questions on the board:

What do you think of the school?

Would you sign up to study there?

Do you think Nicholas has helped or hindered the school's situation?

Have students discuss their ideas in pairs. Then, choose students to share their ideas with the class.

Fast finishers

Students discuss other ways to improve the school's situation.

Work it Out with Phrasal Verbs Work out 8: Business

3

- Have students look at the text in Worksheet 8.1 again. Tell them to find and underline or highlight the phrasal verbs.

5–10 mins

- Have students say how many they found. Explain that there should be 17. Tell students to each come and write a phrasal verb (or more than one, depending on class size) on the board.

PT 8.1

- Put students into pairs. Hand out one copy of **Worksheet 8.2** to each pair (or use **PT 8.1**).

- Ask pairs to match the phrasal verbs from the text to the definitions in the table in Worksheet 8.2. Remind students to read the whole sentence to help them with the meaning of the phrasal verbs.

- Have students read their phrasal verbs and definitions aloud. If projecting, reveal the answers one by one.

Answer key	1 – Sell off	9 – Call in sick
Worksheet 8.2	2 – Be snowed under	10 – Sign up
	3 – Carry out	11 – Rip off
	4 – Take over	12 – Run by
	5 – Take on	13 – Go ahead with
	6 – Get ahead	14 – Note down
	7 – Cut down	15 – Come up with
	8 – Stay behind	16 – Run out
		17 – Call off

Alternative activity
Students find the 17 phrasal verbs in the text (Worksheet 8.1). Put students into pairs. For a more-confident class, have students work independently.
Ask students if they know what an auction is and if they can explain how it works. (An auction is a public sale of goods or property, where people bid (make offers of money) for each item, until it is sold to the person who offers the highest bid.)
'Allocate' £500 to each pair (or individual student). Establish that there's a minimum (£50) and a maximum (£300) bid. The goal is to make as much money as possible by matching phrasal verbs and definitions. On the board, keep track of how much each pair (or student) gains or loses.
Have students read the first definition in Worksheet 8.2. Tell each pair (or student) to place a bid depending on how confident they feel about it (e.g. very confident: £300; not confident: £50). Keep track of all the bids.
Offer students a phrasal verb from the text (Worksheet 8.1), choosing it randomly.
Ask students if they think it's the correct phrasal verb for that definition or not. If the students answer correctly, they double the money from the bid; if their answer is incorrect, they lose their bid.
Repeat the steps for all of the definitions.

4

- Put students into small groups. Explain that each group is a marketing team that will potentially be hired to improve the school's current state. In order to be hired, teams will need to plan and deliver a presentation to the class.

30–40 mins

- Write the following points on the board:

  Student satisfaction

  The school's financial situation

  The location/frontage of the school

  How to market/promote the school better

  How to improve the courses and after-school activities

- Explain that students should try to include these points and any other ideas they might have. Tell them to try to include as many phrasal verbs from the lesson as possible in their presentation.

- For less-confident students, brainstorm ideas as a class before the activity. Give your own ideas if necessary (e.g. school signage should be clear and visible from the main street; organise a weekly social calendar using ideas suggested by students).

Digital alternative

Have students create an infographic, to show the current situation versus what the situation could be like if they used the groups' suggestions, and present it to the class.

Work out 9 — Shopping

'Cinderella is proof that a new pair of shoes can change your life.'

C1

Resources	Worksheet 9.1	one copy per pair
	Worksheet 9.2	one copy per pair
	Worksheet 9.3	one copy per student
	Worksheet 9.4	one copy per student
	Teaching tool 9.1	one teacher copy

Target language

Cough up – to pay someone, usually when you don't want to

Fork out (for something) – to pay more for something than you expected to pay

Knock (something) off – to reduce the price of something by a stated amount

Pick (something) up – to buy something spontaneously

Rip (somebody) off – to make someone pay more than they should

Sell out – to sell all of something; to run out of stock

Shop around (for something) – to compare the price of the same item in different shops

Skimp on (something) – to use too little of something in order to make it last longer

Snap (something) up – to buy something quickly, usually before the stock runs out

Stock up (on something) – to buy a large quantity of something

---

1

o Write the following questions on the board:

How important is money to you?
Why?

How important is money in today's society compared to the past?
Why?

Does the perception of money change depending on whether you live in urban or rural areas?
Why?

o Put students into small groups to discuss the questions.

o Get feedback.

5–10 mins

2

5–10 mins

- Put students into pairs. Give each pair a copy of the cut-up message conversation in **Worksheet 9.1**.

- Ask the class:

  How are the people communicating with each other? (by message)

  How do you know? (informal language, acronyms: OMG)

- Ask students to underline the phrasal verbs they find. Then, have them put the conversation strips in order.

- Get feedback.

Answer key Worksheet 9.1	1 C 2 B 3 D 4 A 5 G 6 E 7 I 8 F 9 H

Alternative activity
Turn this into a timed, competitive activity by setting a short time limit (e.g. three minutes to find the phrasal verbs, three minutes to order the text).

Fast finishers
In pairs, students discuss what they enjoy spending their money on. Give your own ideas if necessary (e.g. clothes, concert tickets, etc.).

3

10–15 mins

- Give each pair a copy of **Worksheet 9.2**. Tell students to look at the first question.

- Ask the class:

  Was it a good performance? (No)

  Was it a good idea to spend money on the tickets for the performance? (No)

- Encourage students to look at Worksheet 9.1 to help them.

- Tell students to write their answers in the correct column.

- Have students look at Worksheet 9.1 again and ask:

  How do you know it wasn't a good idea to spend money on the tickets?

  What words in the text indicate that the money wasn't well spent?

- Elicit answers (e.g. ...glad...didn't...fork out). Have students write their answers in the 'Which words…?' column.

o Ask concept-checking questions (e.g. What are we writing in the 'Which words…?' column? – *the words that help us find the answer to the question*). If necessary, work through the second question together.

o Once completed, students check their answers in pairs.

o Get feedback. Copy or display the Worksheet 9.2 table, and write students' ideas on the board.

Answer key   Worksheet 9.2

Questions	Answers	Which words…?
1. Was the money for the performance well spent?	No	I'm glad you didn't fork out…
2. Was it quick for Kate to buy the camping equipment?	Yes	…snap up all the camping equipment…
3. What did Kate think would happen, because of the sale?	She thought that she wouldn't find any equipment	…it sold out…
4. Did Kate go to many shops to find the best price for her camping equipment?	No	…did you shop around…/…actually I didn't
5. Did she get a discount for the equipment?	Yes	…didn't they knock 30% off the full price
6. Was choosing the equipment difficult for Kate?	No	…picked it up…
7. Did the shop manager try to cheat Kate?	Yes	…tried to rip us off…
8. Would Kate have paid the full price for the equipment?	No	I would have never coughed up all that money…
9. Is Martin going to buy a large or small amount of food and drink for the picnic?	Large	…stock up on…
10. What should Martin buy a lot of?	Food	…don't skimp on what you buy…

4

o Ask students to cover any notes or handouts from the lesson. Divide the class into small groups.

o Tell students to list as many phrasal verbs as they can remember from the previous activity in three minutes. Award points for correct answers. The winning team is the group that remembers the most.

15–20 mins

PT 9.1

- Give a copy of **Worksheet 9.3** to each student (or use **PT 9.1**). Have students complete the questions using the phrasal verbs from the previous activity (Worksheet 9.2). Remind students to think about the tense they need to use. For less-confident students, provide access to the worksheet's Phrasal Verb box.

- Get feedback.

- Have students discuss the questions in pairs, and encourage them to explain the reasons for their answers.

- Have one or two pairs share what they discussed with the class.

Answer key	1. ripped off	4. skimp on	7. stock up
Worksheet 9.3	2. coughed up/forked out	5. sold out	8. knock off
	3. pick up	6. shop around	9. snapped up

Extension

Tell students to walk around the class and to speak to their classmates. Encourage them to ask a different question to a different student each time.

Choose one or two students to share what they heard with the class.

Digital tip

Students write the interview questions on an online survey-maker platform (e.g. SurveyMonkey). Have each student send their survey to three or four classmates to complete. Have students write a short summary of their findings to share in the next lesson.

5
- Give each student a copy of **Worksheet 9.4** and ask them the following questions:

    What type of text is this? (A review)

    What is it reviewing? (A tent)

    Is it a positive or negative review? How do you know? (positive; the language used)

    How many paragraphs are there? (Four)

- Explain that a review can be positive or negative, depending on a person's experience of something.

- Ask students to read the review and to make a note of what each paragraph includes (e.g. Para 1 – an introduction to the product; Para 2 – the advantages of it; etc.).

15–20 mins

- o Put students into pairs to compare their notes. Encourage them to underline or highlight the phrasal verbs that are used.

- o Elicit the structure of a review as a class (see **Teaching tool 9.1**).

Teaching tool 9.1			
Paragraph	**Purpose**	**Features**	**Phrasal Verbs**
1 (Introduction)	Introducing the product and the reviewer	Engaging question Imperative tenses (e.g. Look no further)	snap up, sell out
2 (Main body)	Describing aspects and qualities of the product	Adjectives/adverbs (e.g. lightweight, waterproof/easily)	pick up
3 (Main body)	Describing size and storage	Number of people Nouns (e.g. wardrobe, pockets)	skimp on, stock up
4 (Conclusion)	Price and service	Related vocabulary (e.g. cheap, bargain, delivery)	shop around, fork out, knock off, pick up

6

- o Tell students that they are now going to write a review (between 150 and 250 words) about an item they have bought. Write the following on the board:

25–30 mins

Something you managed to buy at a very low price

A product you're particularly happy/unhappy with

- o Ask the class: *Is a review formal or informal?* (informal)

- o They should use the phrasal verbs from the lesson in their reviews.

- o To provide further support for the writing, write the following questions on the board:

<u>Introduction</u>: *What item was it? Was it a popular/fashionable item? What did you need it for?*

<u>Main body</u>: *What happened before you went to buy it? What happened when you were buying (or trying to buy) it? What happened after you bought it?*

<u>Conclusion</u>: *Were you happy with the shopping experience? Why? Why not? What advice would you give to any potential buyer of the same product?*

- o Have students make notes on the item they will review, using the questions to prompt them.

- Have students discuss their notes and their product in pairs. Have one or two students share their ideas with the class.

- Once students have completed their writing, have them swap with their partners and read each other's reviews. Encourage them to use a pencil to highlight any errors they think they find.

- Have pairs correct any errors from their partner. Provide assistance as necessary.

Fast finishers

In pairs, students read each other's review. Have each student write:

- one specific positive comment about their partner's review (e.g. the use of a range of adjectives)

- one comment about something that could be improved (e.g. forgetting to use phrasal verbs).

Encourage students to give reasons for their comments.

Work out 10 — Health

'The greatest wealth is health.'

B2+

Resources	Worksheet 10.1 one copy per pair
	Worksheet 10.2 one copy per pair
	Worksheet 10.3 one copy per pair

Target language

Block up – to stop something moving through something else

Break out – when you develop a sudden skin irritation

Build up (your strength) – to slowly become stronger after an illness

Come down with (an illness) – to become ill with an illness that is not very serious

Fight off – to attempt to free yourself from an illness

Get over – to recover from an illness

Pass away – to die

Pass out – to lose consciousness; to faint

Pick (something) up – to catch a non-serious illness from another person or place

Throw up – to vomit

1
- Act out that you're feeling unwell (e.g. coughing, fainting, etc.).
- Ask students the following questions and elicit answers:

    What do you think is happening to me? (you're ill)

    What symptoms do you recognise? (cough, fainting)

    What should I do? (go to the doctor, take medication etc.)

- Put students into pairs and ask them to draw a table with two columns: *Positives* and *Negatives*.
- Hand out one copy of **Worksheet 10.1** to each student (or you could use **PT 10.1**). Ask students to read the sentences, and to decide if the phrasal verbs sound positive or negative. Have students put them in the correct column.
- Get feedback. Invite students to come and write their ideas on the board. Do not confirm answers at this point.

5–10 mins

PT 10.1

Work it Out with Phrasal Verbs   Work out 10: Health

Answer key Worksheet 10.1	Positives: 3, 5, 8 (8 could also be negative)
	Negatives: 1, 2, 4, 6, 7, 8, 9, 10

> **Digital alternative**
>
> Display the sentences in PT 10.1 one-by-one on screen for the class to see.
>
> Students write 'P' (positive) and 'N' (negative) in large writing on either side of a piece of paper.
>
> For each sentence displayed, students hold up 'P' or 'N' depending on whether they think the phrasal verbs sound positive or negative. Note: some phrasal verbs can be positive **and** negative.

2
- Put students in pairs. Hand out **Worksheet 10.2** to each pair.
- Ask students to highlight the phrasal verbs that appear.
- Ask students to read the text and discuss, in their pairs, whether they still agree with the positive and negative phrasal verbs. Avoid discussing definitions at this point.
- Get class feedback.

5–10 mins

3
- Put students in pairs. Hand out **Worksheet 10.3** to each pair.
- Ask students to read the definitions and to complete the gaps using the phrasal verbs identified in Worksheet 10.2.
- Get feedback. Clarify any definitions as necessary.

5–10 mins

Answer key Worksheet 10.3	A – came down with	F – getting over
	B – build up	G – throw up
	C – fight off	H – pass out
	D – break out	I – passed away
	E – blocked up	J – picked up

4
- On one side of the board, draw two columns titled: *Minor Health Problems* and *Treatments*.
- Put students in small groups. Have them brainstorm minor health issues (e.g. headaches, coughing, etc.).

10–15 mins

- o Ask groups to share their ideas with the class. Write their ideas in the correct column on the board.

- o Repeat the steps for *Treatments*. Have students brainstorm, then write their answers on the board. Give examples if necessary (e.g. drink herbal tea (for a stomach ache); take a tablet/pill (for a headache); raise your legs (for passing out/fainting); etc.). Encourage students to use phrasal verbs learnt throughout the lesson (e.g. pass out; build up strength; etc.).

5

- o Leave the text from the previous activity on the board. Next to this, write: *Dialogue Outline*.

5–10 mins

- o Ask the class: *What is a dialogue?* (a conversation).

- o Tell students to imagine they are visiting a doctor. Ask: *What would be the first thing you'd say?* (Hello/Hi/Hey, etc.)

- o Write *Greetings* on the board under the title *Dialogue Outline*. Then, ask the class what they think would likely be discussed in an appointment with a doctor. Write students' ideas on the board. Prompt the class if necessary (e.g. asking what's wrong; explaining symptoms; giving a diagnosis; giving reassurance, etc.).

- o Put students into small groups to think of what expressions/phrases/vocabulary they could use for each point. For example: *What's wrong?/What's the matter?*; *I've had a headache for a while*; *You might likely have/be…*; *If I were you, I would…*; *Why don't you…?*; etc.

- o Students share their ideas with the class.

- o For less-confident classes, write students' ideas on the board to prompt them in the next activity. For more-confident classes, do not write students' ideas on the board.

6

- o Divide the class into two groups. Organise the classroom so the seats are facing each other. If in a smaller space, have students stand opposite each other in two circles – one facing the interior of the classroom and one facing the exterior.

25–30 mins

- o Tell students that they are going to the doctor to discuss an issue they have been having. Assign students as A and B. Tell As that they are the doctor, and Bs that they are the patient with the health issue. Tell them to use the language on the board to help them with their dialogue.

Work it Out with Phrasal Verbs   Work out 10: Health

- o   Encourage students to use as many phrasal verbs from the lesson as they can. Set a visible timer of four minutes. Once the time is up, have B's move to speak to the student on their left, so they are speaking to a new 'doctor'. Encourage them to think of a new health problem to describe.

- o   Once students have spoken to two doctors, switch roles – As become the patient and Bs become the doctor. Repeat the steps.

- o   Ask students to share which problems and treatments they heard. Encourage them to say which phrasal verbs they used.

Extension

Write the following on the board:

Dizziness, a fever, sore eyes

A cough, sneezing, loss of voice

Itchy arms and legs

Earache, toothache, a rash on your cheek

Put students into small groups. Tell them that they are going to choose one of the sets of symptoms on the board to share with their classmates, who will give them some advice on how to treat it. They can then choose the best advice to take.

Have each group write their symptoms and issues in a short paragraph. Encourage students to use the phrasal verbs (e.g. I've come down with something, and I need your help. I've broken out in a rash on my cheek and I've had a pounding earache for about a week.).

Have groups take it in turns to present their issue to the class. Have the class suggest some treatments to the groups, for them to choose the best advice.

Have less-confident groups present their issue to another group.

Worksheets

Work it Out with Phrasal Verbs

Worksheets 1.1 & 1.2

✂

Worksheet 1.1

Julia, 19

I recently went shopping with my friend and, when my back was turned, I noticed that she'd put some expensive makeup in her bag. At first, I thought it was simply a mistake, but after I'd paid for my things, I realised she hadn't paid for hers. I didn't say anything to her, but now I think I should tell someone, like a manager, who works in the shop. What should I do? Help!

Aida, 41

For most of my adult life, I've worked really hard and made a huge effort to be the best at what I do. For the past three years I've worked for the same company and have put in a lot of extra time working weekends and late evenings, as well as doing my colleagues' work that they can't manage. On one hand, I think I should continue working as hard as I have been because it's the way I am and I'm determined to get a promotion, but, on the other hand, maybe I should just quit my job and find a company that appreciates me, or at least pays me for my extra time.

Jack, 28

Oh my gosh! I'm so angry! Help me! You won't believe what happened to me recently. I had a really painful toothache, so I made an appointment with the dentist to have a look at my teeth. I told them over the phone what my problem was and they said I needed quite a big operation. I paid for it over the phone so I could go in, have it done, then leave feeling better straight away. Unfortunately, I had to wait a bit longer. After a week of pain, I finally got to the dental clinic to find it had shut down! They had accepted my payment and gone! I'm furious! How can I get my money back? Help!

....

Worksheet 1.2

A   In my opinion, you should continue to put in time and effort but make sure you speak to someone in a higher position than you. Arrange a meeting with a senior member of staff and, politely, mention your concerns. If this still doesn't help the situation, start looking for a new job in a higher position and apply for something that suits your skillset and offers career-development opportunities. Try to speak to people you know and see if their companies are hiring as well. Hope this helps!

B   First of all, you should take a deep breath and relax. In this case you should take a look at getting some legal advice, depending on the amount of money you paid. Alternatively, you could just forget about it, move on and find a new place to go in future. You need to be less angry and be happy!

C   It's a tricky situation. I don't think you should say anything – but then, if you don't, maybe that person won't reflect on what they've done and won't learn a lesson and might continue to do it! I wouldn't want to be in your shoes…

Work it Out with Phrasal Verbs

Worksheet 1.3

1	check out	A	To become, or make somebody become, less excited, anxious or upset
2	speak up	B	To be sure you are going to achieve the objective you have in mind
3	keep on	C	To take a look at something
4	take on	D	To continue doing something
5	calm down	E	To reflect on something
6	think over	F	To express opinions freely and honestly
7	cheer up	G	To begin, or take responsibility for, something
8	set on (doing something)	H	To speak to many people to find an answer
9	look into (something)	I	To make yourself, or someone else, feel happier
10	ask around	J	To do research to find something

Work it Out with Phrasal Verbs

Worksheet 1.4

	Phrasal verb	Problem Worksheet 1.1	Phrase	Response Worksheet 1.2	Phrase
1	check out				
2	speak up				
3	keep on				
4	take on				
5	calm down			B	*Take a deep breath and relax*
6	think over				
7	cheer up				
8	set on (doing something)				
9	look into				
10	ask around				

Work it Out with Phrasal Verbs

Worksheet 2.1

	A	B	C
1	split up	look up to her	tell her off
2	look like	grow up	bring up
3	grew up	split up	got on with
4	split up	fall out	look up to
5	look like	get on with	look after
6	fell out	looked like	brought up
7	bringing up	looking up to	telling off
8	fall out	get on	look like
9	looked after	split up	grew up

	A	B	C
1	split up	look up to her	tell her off
2	look like	grow up	bring up
3	grew up	split up	got on with
4	split up	fall out	look up to
5	look like	get on with	look after
6	fell out	looked like	brought up
7	bringing up	looking up to	telling off
8	fall out	get on	look like
9	looked after	split up	grew up

Work it Out with Phrasal Verbs

Worksheet 3.1

A	I can't wait to go...	1	...in until 2pm.
B	My boss said I can take some...	2	...off, I get so nervous!
C	It's early. We can't check...	3	...out – no cooking and no washing up!
D	I'm bored! I hate waiting...	4	...out time is 11am.
E	Hold my hand! When the plane takes...	5	...away for a week. It'll be great!
F	It's time to go. The check...	6	...in a taxi before we get wet.
G	It's raining! Let's get...	7	...around for my luggage.
H	So many restaurants! I love eating...	8	...time off before the summer.

Work it Out with Phrasal Verbs

Worksheet 3.2

Team A

	Question	Name and answer	Name and answer
1	How often do you go away on holiday?		
2	What do you do when you take some time off?		
3	When you eat out, what kind of food do you usually choose? Why?		
4	When you're waiting around for someone or something, how do you kill time?		
5	How do you feel while the plane is taking off or landing?		
6	Have you ever had problems when checking in to or out of a hotel?		
7	How long would you wait around for a friend who is late?		
8	Have you ever got into the wrong car by accident?		

Work it Out with Phrasal Verbs

Worksheet 3.3

Team B

	Question	Name and answer	Name and answer
1	When did you last go away on holiday? Where did you go?		
2	How do you feel when you're waiting around for someone who's late?		
3	What is there for people to do in your country when they take time off work?		
4	What is the earliest you've ever set off on holiday? Where did you go?		
5	What do you prefer – when the plane takes off or when it lands?		
6	Have you ever been too early to check in or too late to check out?		
7	What do you do when you're hanging around at the airport?		
8	Have you ever walked into a hotel room and then asked to change? Why? If not, would you?		

Work it Out with Phrasal Verbs

Worksheet 4.1

✂

....

D I met a girl through a friend, who I got on really well with. We had similar interests, and a similar perspective on life.

....

A I was feeling confident one day after we had been messaging for a few weeks, so I decided to ask her out.

....

C Our first date was a romantic dinner and we immediately hit it off. We stayed for hours, just talking and enjoying each other's company.

....

B After five or six dates, I was really starting to fall for her. We had so much in common and always had such fun together.

....

E We have now been together for more than five years and are settling down. We've recently bought our first house together!

....

Work it Out with Phrasal Verbs

Worksheet 4.2

✂

C I met a boy at work who was always smiling and flirting with me, and we organised a first date. I waited at the restaurant for an hour, and he stood me up! He didn't come!

E The next day at work he asked me out again, to go for dinner that evening, but I was so angry I turned him down. He continued to ask me every day for a week, until I finally said yes.

D One night, we had dinner and had a lot to talk about. We started to go on three or four dates per week and started a relationship. But after one month, we had a big argument and split up.

A I missed him so much that, three days after our fight, we made up.

B We had another big argument the same week after we got back together, and now he is with someone else. He was just leading me on for something to do with his evenings! We've definitely split up for good this time!

Work it Out with Phrasal Verbs

Worksheet 4.3

Extension

Relationships

Across

2. To make someone think you are interested in them but you are not
4. To invite someone to go out with you
7. To have an instant connection with someone
9. To start a family and have children

Down

1. To become friends after having an argument
3. To begin to love someone
5. To have a good relationship with someone
6. If someone arranges to meet you and they don't come
8. To end a relationship
10. To say no to an invitation to go out

Work it Out with Phrasal Verbs

Worksheet 4.4

	Find someone who…	Name of student / Notes
1	has been asked out	
2	has fallen for someone quickly	
3	has broken up with someone	
4	has been stood up by a friend	
5	has hit it off with someone instantly	
6	wants to settle down soon	
7	finds it difficult to make up with people	
8	has been turned down in the last few months by a friend.	

Work it Out with Phrasal Verbs

Worksheets 5.1 & 5.2

✂

Worksheet 5.1

Group A

The Dos and Don'ts at meal times

Many agree that, in order to keep in good health and to avoid putting on weight, it would be a good idea to follow specific rules.

1. You should pick at food rather than have complete meals.
2. It is also believed that food high in saturated fats should be cut out from your diet if your goal is to be healthy.
3. It is suggested that you eat small portions of carbohydrates because this might fill you up quickly and stop you eating more.
4. Eating out and ordering food to take away too often leads to overeating and weight gain.
5. You should eat slowly. Wolfing down your food is bad for your digestive system.

....

Worksheet 5.2

Group B

The Dos and Don'ts at meal times

Food and health advice might help you stay in shape. However, I personally believe that it could cause frustration and stress, which might lead to other food-related issues. So, here are my top tips for enjoying your food without affecting your health.

1. Try to enjoy cooking and eating in. Invite your friends over and serve up a tasty meal – sharing is caring!
2. Ask your friends to contribute to your meal by bringing some nice drinks to wash it down.
3. Avoid food that disagrees with you: be aware of any allergies or intolerances that you or your guests may have.
4. Always check your ingredients before cooking to make sure they haven't gone off.
5. If you aren't keen on cooking, you can order some pizza, slice it up and let your friends help themselves to as many pieces as they want.
6. And my final (non-health-related!) tip is to remember to top up your friends' glasses – and yours – if you want to be a good host.

Work it Out with Phrasal Verbs

Worksheet 5.3

Complete the sentences with the phrasal verbs in the box.

cut out	pick at	fill up	eat out
wolf down	eat in	serve up	wash down	go off
slice up	top up	put on	take away

1   Marco wasn't hungry; he could only _____ his food.

2   Your glass is nearly empty. Shall I _____ it _____?

3   You should eat slowly and enjoy your food. You shouldn't _____ it _____!

4   Maria _____ her birthday cake to share with her friends.

5   The doctor told me to _____ fast food from my diet if I want to stay healthy.

6   I love to _____. I enjoy cooking for my friends and family and it's cheaper than going to a restaurant.

7   On a hot day, I like to _____ my food with a nice cold drink.

8   I don't like cooking and restaurants are expensive, so I often order some food that I can _____ and eat at home.

9   When we _____, I always order something I wouldn't cook at home.

10 Milk smells so bad when it has _____!

11 My friend is such a good cook! She always _____ delicious meals.

12 Since I stopped going to the gym, I've _____ a lot of weight.

13 Burgers and chips taste amazing, but they _____ me _____ so much!

Work it Out with Phrasal Verbs

Worksheet 6.1

Key elements of dreams

1	Gym	
2	Joining a class/a course/an activity	
3	Short visit to a friend	
4	Meeting a friend for a chat after a long time	
5	Improvise a meal	
6	Spending the night in somebody else's house	
7	Others doing exercise	
8	Reading a contract carefully	
9	Paying by debit card	
10	Debit card stuck to hand	

Key elements of dreams

1	Gym	
2	Joining a class/a course/an activity	
3	Short visit to a friend	
4	Meeting a friend for a chat after a long time	
5	Improvise a meal	
6	Spending the night in somebody else's house	
7	Others doing exercise	
8	Reading a contract carefully	
9	Paying by debit card	
10	Debit card stuck to hand	

Work it Out with Phrasal Verbs

Worksheet 6.2

Dream definitions

A Dreaming about looking at other people working out might mean that you feel frustration for not achieving your own goals, while others seem accomplished.

B Catching up with friends in a dream might reveal that you need to clarify misunderstandings and solve issues in your life.

C Dreaming of sleeping over at someone's house could mean that you need to improve your social life or that you're avoiding an uncomfortable situation.

D Dreaming of popping over to a friend's house could mean that you need to reconnect with your loved ones (friends or family).

E When you dream of thoroughly reading a contract, going over every clause and detail before signing it, this might mean that you are unsure of the commitments in your life.

F Credit or debit cards often appear in dreams. This might mean that you're anxious about your responsibilities. So, dreaming about paying by card could indicate the effort involved in being responsible in your daily life.

G Dreaming about a gym could mean the need to include more physical activity in your daily routine. Your body is trying to tell you that your life is not active enough.

H Holding a credit or debit card in your dreams is a good sign: your business will be successful, or your career will progress. However, if you can't let go of your card, this dream could mean that you're hiding parts of your personality. Just like an onion, you need to peel off the layers to reveal your true self to the people who are closest to you.

I If you dream of someone cooking a meal for you, it might suggest that you need emotional support. Depending on the meal being cooked, the dream has different meanings: breakfast represents a trap, lunch indicates career progression, and dinner might alert of the influence of negative thoughts in your mind.

J Dreaming about signing up for a class means that you have professional or personal goals that you want to achieve and you are ready to work for them.

Work it Out with Phrasal Verbs

Worksheet 6.3

Dream 1

"Last week I dreamt that I had signed up to two language courses, a carpentry course, and a horse riding course. With so many activities, I was so busy that I couldn't find the time to see my friends. What do you think this dream means?"

Dream 2

"Last night I woke up screaming in the middle of the night because I had a terrible nightmare: I had 30 young children sleeping over at my house and I had to look after them... It was crazy!"

Dream 3

"I keep having a dream about handing over the keys to my house to a complete stranger. I always wake up feeling very anxious. What could this dream mean?"

Dream 4

"What a stressful dream! I received a phone call from my mother-in-law telling me that she was coming over for dinner with her five friends. What's worse is that she was going to be there in ten minutes! I immediately rushed to the kitchen to rustle something up..."

Dream 5

"The night before my final exam was very stressful. I couldn't relax, and when I finally fell asleep I had the worst dream ever: I was in the exam room by myself going over my notes, trying to memorise a lot of information, but nothing would stick in my mind. When I woke up I was exhausted!"

Dream 6

"Last summer I got sunburnt and my skin was really sore. During the night, I must have been in agony because I dreamt that my skin was peeling off and it wouldn't stop! It was petrifying!"

Dream 7

"The most ridiculous dream I've ever had was about the Queen who popped over to mine for a cup of tea... What was going on in my head that night?!?"

Dream 8

"When I first joined a gym I was really excited about getting fit. Once I dreamt about working out for ten hours non-stop! The morning after I was shattered..."

Dream 9

"When I was in primary school, I had a crush on a boy. I've recently dreamt about messaging him to catch up with him, even though I haven't seen him since my school days."

Dream 10

"My weirdest dream was about a safe that I'd been given and I had to figure out the combination by doing a series of challenges in order to open it."

Work it Out with Phrasal Verbs

Worksheet 7.1

A

Panic Package!

Last night, after what appeared to be a break in, a mysterious package blew up in the front lawn of a local resident on South Street. Detectives think it was a notorious inmate who had broken out of Sumberdown Prison.

B

Motorway Fight

At 10pm last Thursday evening, a car was seen speeding at 120mph along a busy motorway. The police pulled the driver over, but an altercation ensued. The driver knocked out one of the police officers….

C

'MOST WANTED': FINALLY FOUND

An infamous criminal, who the police had been hunting for months, today turned himself in. 17 years earlier, he had been put on the 'Most Wanted Fugitives' list, for attempting to set fire to a disused hospital. The criminal has managed to get away with the crime for over a decade.

D

THE MOST CRIMINAL PLACE IN THE CITY

Andrew Penfold, Saturday 12th May

A criminal gang has been found guilty and locked up for selling illegal and stolen items. Two of the younger gang members were let off. Detectives spent hours staking out the comings and goings of an apartment block in the downtown area before they finally arrested the group.

Work it Out with Phrasal Verbs

Worksheet 7.2

✂

Story A

2. There was a man who was down on his luck, so he decided to rob a bank to earn some easy money.

6. He chose a Monday morning. He covered his face, took a baseball bat, and went to the bank.

3. When he was asking the bank clerk for the money, he didn't expect that someone would jump on his back and he would have to fight them until they were unconscious!

1. He escaped with the money and ran as fast as he could to his car.

5. He started to drive so fast that when he looked in the mirror he saw flashing blue lights and the police signalling for him to move to the side of the road.

4. He was put into prison for 180 days, but some people believe he should have got a longer sentence.

. . . .

Story B

3. A woman had been in prison mistakenly for more than ten years, for a crime she didn't commit. The police offered her freedom in exchange for information about another crime. She offered details about the crime John committed.

1. After she spoke to the police, she realised they didn't believe her. She decided she had no option but to escape from prison.

4. For her to do this, she first had to create an explosion at the entrance of her cell. At the same time, she needed to create a loud sound as a distraction.

6. She asked the woman on the floor below to scream at the top of her voice, so that the guards couldn't hear the bang.

5. The morning of the escape, fortunately, she was able to plead her innocence with the judges.

2. That day, she was told she could go free on one condition: that she helped the police by sitting outside John's house to find the evidence of his wrongdoing.

Work it Out with Phrasal Verbs

Worksheet 7.3

Scorecard: Group A

How many members of the group spoke? ☐

Examples of advanced vocabulary:

[   ]

Score: | 1 | 2 | 3 | 4 | 5 | *1 = Could be improved   5 = Excellent*

Examples of grammatical/pronunciation errors:

[   ]

Winner of round: | Group A | Group B |

Scorecard: Group B

How many members of the group spoke? ☐

Examples of advanced vocabulary:

[   ]

Score: | 1 | 2 | 3 | 4 | 5 | *1 = Could be improved   5 = Excellent*

Examples of grammatical/pronunciation errors:

[   ]

Winner of round: | Group A | Group B |

Work it Out with Phrasal Verbs

Worksheet 8.1

Case Study: English Fluency Ltd.

English Fluency Ltd. is a private language school for students of English as a second language based in Newport, UK. The School Director, Nicholas Cooper, took over the role ten months ago, when the previous director retired. Cooper's contract runs out in two months' time, but he's hoping that it will be renewed at the end of next month during his appraisal.

During the last three months, several complaints have been received from students who claim to have been ripped off by the school concerning their new courses. They are not happy with how many lessons per day they receive for the amount of money they have paid, and they object to the lack of extra-curricular activities, which the students have continually asked for. This has meant that the number of students is rapidly declining.

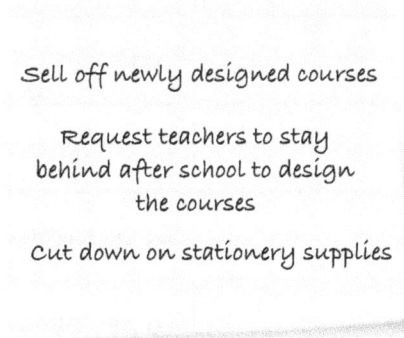

The School Director's notes

In addition, teachers have been snowed under with work and have frequently called in sick as they can't handle the workload and are not being paid enough for the number of hours they are working.

This has led to many teachers now leaving, causing a very high turnover of staff, and the remaining teachers are being underpaid. Because of the lack of students, the school is struggling financially. As well as this, the front of the school is very hidden, situated off of the main street, meaning it is difficult to promote the school to members of the public, and the school currently has no marketing budget.

In order to try and improve the situation, the school has decided to carry out a survey to assess the level of dissatisfaction among teachers and students. This, however, is not enough to improve the ever-decreasing student sign-up numbers.

Questions:

1. What type of business is English Fluency Ltd., and what are the issues?

2. What does the text say about the School Director?

3. What ideas are listed in his plan?

4. What were the consequences of his plan?

Work it Out with Phrasal Verbs

Worksheet 8.2

	Phrasal verbs	Meaning
1		To sell something at a lower price because you need the money
2		To have a lot of work to do
3		To do or complete a task
4		To replace someone in their role
5		To employ someone
6		To be successful in your job
7		To decrease the quantity of something used
8		To not leave a place (school/work) when other people leave
9		To inform your workplace that you are too sick to work
10		To subscribe or to join a group or a course
11		To cheat someone by charging them too much money for something
12		To share your ideas with someone to hear their opinion
13		To start doing something after waiting for someone's permission
14		To write something down to avoid forgetting it
15		To think of something, such as an idea or a plan
16		When something comes to an end, such as a contract or an agreement
17		To stop something from happening, such as a wedding or a meeting

Work it Out with Phrasal Verbs

Worksheet 9.1

✂

C   Hey Kate, how's you? How was the festival?

B   OMG Martin!! It was a disaster! I'm so glad you didn't fork out all that money for such a terrible weekend...

D   Yeah… It wasn't cheap, was it?! Anyway, the atmosphere must've been great either way and you must have enjoyed the camping experience, right?

A   Yeah, I really enjoyed it – it was my first time sleeping in a tent! We were lucky enough to snap up all the camping equipment before it sold out and we got a great deal because the manager knocked 30% off of the full price, as the tent was on display!

G   Wow! So you didn't have to shop around for something cheaper – what a bargain!

E   Well, actually, we did go to a few places first before we eventually got what we needed. In one shop, the manager tried (and failed) to rip us off – he "forgot" there was a sale on and wanted to charge me full price!! I'd never have coughed up all that money for some camping gear!

I   Yeah… after all, how often are you gonna use it? You'd never get your money's worth. Anyway, I gotta go – going shopping now. I need to stock up on food and drinks for our picnic on Sunday!

F   Of course… and don't skimp on what you buy! Remember I had loads of food when I hosted the last one! See you on Sunday then xx

H   See u!

Work it Out with Phrasal Verbs

Worksheet 9.2

	Questions	Answers	Which words…?
1	Was the money for the performance well spent?		
2	Was it quick and easy for Kate to buy the camping equipment?		
3	What did Kate think would happen after the sale?		
4	Did Kate go to many shops to find the best price for her camping equipment?		
5	Did she get a discount for the equipment?		
6	Was choosing the equipment difficult for Kate?		
7	Did the shop manager try to cheat Kate?		
8	Would Kate have paid the full price for the equipment?		
9	Is Martin going to buy a large or small amount of food and drink for the picnic?		
10	What should Martin buy a lot of?		

Work it Out with Phrasal Verbs

Worksheet 9.3

1. Have you ever been _____ or cheated in a shop?

2. Have you ever _____ a large amount of money for an unpleasant reason?

3. How often do you _____ a new pair of shoes even if you don't need them?

4. What do you _____ when you want to save money?

5. Have you ever had the intention of buying something only to realise that the shop had _____ of it when you got there?

6. Do you usually buy on impulse or do you _____ to find the best deal?

7. When it comes to food shopping, what do you usually _____ on?

8. Have you ever persuaded someone to _____ some money from the full price of something you bought?

9. Have you ever _____ the last item in stock?

Phrasal verb box (optional)

Rip (somebody) off	Shop around (for something)	Snap (something) up
Stock up (on something)	Fork out (for something)	
Sell out	Skimp on (something)	Cough up
Knock (something) off (something)		Pick (something) up

Work it Out with Phrasal Verbs

Worksheet 9.4

Are you looking for the ideal tent for your outdoor adventures? Look no further, you've found it!

I'm a camping enthusiast and I've bought several tents in the past twenty years, but EazyTent™ is by far the best one I've ever had. I'm happy I've snapped it up before it sells out!

A tent isn't an item you just pick up during a regular shopping trip – it requires serious consideration. EazyTent™ is lightweight and aesthetically appealing. It can be easily folded and fits in the waterproof backpack provided. The tent itself is waterproof and comes in three different colours: green, orange, or brown. The real surprise is its see-through roof, which is perfect for stargazing. This durable, sturdy tent is available in two models, to accommodate four or eight people. Regardless of the size you need, EazyTent™ is easy to put together, even just for one person, and it's very spacious. It doesn't skimp on storage either, boasting a foldable wardrobe and plenty of pockets if you want to stock up on food and drinks!

Such wonderful features don't come cheap, and you might be tempted to shop around for a bargain. Well, don't bother. If you don't want to fork out the full price for EazyTent™, order it directly from the website and they'll knock 10% off! You can have your tent delivered to your door or collect it at one of their warehouses – you couldn't ask for a better service!

Work it Out with Phrasal Verbs

Worksheet 10.1

✂

1. I've *come down with* the flu so I'm unable to work today.
2. I *picked up* a cold from the air conditioning!
3. I'm trying to *build up* my strength by eating fruit and taking vitamins.
4. This morning, I *threw up* my dinner from last night.
5. I'm finally *getting over* the cold I've had for ages.
6. My nose is so *blocked up*! I need more tissues!
7. Amina suddenly *passed out*.
8. I *fought off* that terrible fever by resting for a few days.
9. Juan suddenly *broke out* in lots of spots!
10. Unfortunately, Uncle David *passed away* last night.

- -

1. I've *come down with* the flu so I'm unable to work today.
2. I *picked up* a cold from the air conditioning!
3. I'm trying to *build up* my strength by eating fruit and taking vitamins.
4. This morning, I *threw up* my dinner from last night.
5. I'm finally *getting over* the cold I've had for ages.
6. My nose is so *blocked up*! I need more tissues!
7. Amina suddenly *passed out*.
8. I *fought off* that terrible fever by resting for a few days.
9. Juan suddenly *broke out* in lots of spots!
10. Unfortunately, Uncle David *passed away* last night.

Work it Out with Phrasal Verbs

Worksheet 10.2

✂

I had a terrible week last week. I've been trying to build up my strength since I came down with the flu; it lasted two whole weeks! I picked it up from a holiday I went on, a cruise around the Mediterranean, but I spent most of the time throwing up and my nose was blocked up. I even passed out once! It all started when I broke out in a rash on my arm, which I think was caused by a bite, and then the air conditioning was left on when I slept – what a nightmare! I came back on Tuesday. I fought off my cold and am finally getting over my illness. I came home to unfortunate news though – my uncle had passed away while I was abroad. Well, they do say bad things happen in threes.

....

I had a terrible week last week. I've been trying to build up my strength since I came down with the flu; it lasted two whole weeks! I picked it up from a holiday I went on, a cruise around the Mediterranean, but I spent most of the time throwing up and my nose was blocked up. I even passed out once! It all started when I broke out in a rash on my arm, which I think was caused by a bite, and then the air conditioning was left on when I slept – what a nightmare! I came back on Tuesday. I fought off my cold and am finally getting over my illness. I came home to unfortunate news though – my uncle had passed away while I was abroad. Well, they do say bad things happen in threes.

....

I had a terrible week last week. I've been trying to build up my strength since I came down with the flu; it lasted two whole weeks! I picked it up from a holiday I went on, a cruise around the Mediterranean, but I spent most of the time throwing up and my nose was blocked up. I even passed out once! It all started when I broke out in a rash on my arm, which I think was caused by a bite, and then the air conditioning was left on when I slept – what a nightmare! I came back on Tuesday. I fought off my cold and am finally getting over my illness. I came home to unfortunate news though – my uncle had passed away while I was abroad. Well, they do say bad things happen in threes.

Work it Out with Phrasal Verbs

Worksheet 10.3

A	**Phrasal verb:** _____ **Definition:** *Started to become ill*	**B**	**Phrasal verb:** _____ **Definition:** *To slowly increase*
C	**Phrasal verb:** _____ **Definition:** *No longer ill, because you tried hard to overcome it*	**D**	**Phrasal verb:** _____ **Definition:** *Suddenly appeared*
E	**Phrasal verb:** _____ **Definition:** *Difficulty in breathing*	**F**	**Phrasal verb:** _____ **Definition:** *To recover*
G	**Phrasal verb:** _____ **Definition:** *To vomit*	**H**	**Phrasal verb:** _____ **Definition:** *To lose consciousness/to faint*
I	**Phrasal verb:** _____ **Definition:** *Died*	**J**	**Phrasal verb:** _____ **Definition:** *Caught*

Extra practice

Work it Out with Phrasal Verbs   Extra practice

1 Extra practice 1: Advice

   o   Cut up and shuffle the cards. Give a set to each pair of students.   10–15 mins

   o   Students match verbs and particles to create phrasal verbs from this lesson only.

   o   Students match each phrasal verb to its synonym and definition.

2 Extra practice 2: Family

   o   Students match pictures 1–9 to sentences A–I.   10–15 mins

   o   Then, students write their own sentences using the pictures to help them.

Answer key	1 D 2 E 3 A 4 H 5 B 6 F 7 G 8 I 9 C

3 Extra practice 3: Holidays

   o   In pairs, allocate one set of role-play cards – one card per student.   20–25 mins

   o   Students use phrasal verbs from the lesson in their conversation.

   o   Once finished, students exchange sets of cards and repeat the previous three steps.

4 Extra practice 4: Relationships

   o   In A and B pairs, students describe their phrasal verb to their partner, without saying any of the words or phrases on the card.   10–15 mins

   o   Students have three guesses for each phrasal verb. The student that guesses the most correctly at the end of the game wins.

5 Extra practice 5: Eating and drinking

   o   Students choose the correct phrasal verb to complete the sentences.   15–20 mins

   o   In small groups, students discuss whether they agree or disagree with the statements and why.

Work it Out with Phrasal Verbs — Extra practice

| Answer key | 1 gone off; 2 cut out; 3 eat out; eat in; 4 pick at; 5 wolf down; 6 take away | 7 top up; 8 wash down; 9 sliced up; 10 put on; 11 fill myself up; 12 serving up |

6 Extra practice 6: Dreams

10–15 mins

○ Students read the definitions. They choose the verb to match the definition, then complete it with the missing particle.

Answer key	1 E – Catch **up**	6 J – Peel (something) **off**
	2 B – Hand **over** (something)	7 G – Sleep **over**
	3 H – Work **out**	8 F – Sign **up for** (something)
	4 I – Figure **out**	9 D – Go **over** (something)
	5 A – Pop **over**	10 C – Rustle (something) **up**

7 Extra practice 7: Crime

15–20 mins

○ Students complete the newspaper stories with the correct phrasal verbs, using the pictures to help them.

Answer key	7a:	7b:
	1 locked up	1 blown up
	2 broke into	2 broke out of
	3 got away with	3 knocked out
	4 pulled over	4 staking out
	5 let off	5 turn themselves in

8 Extra practice 8: Business

25–30 mins

○ Align students in two rows (A and B) facing each other. Give each row a set of questions.

○ Students interview different classmates in a 'speed-dating' fashion. Every student stands opposite someone; if there is an odd number of students, the teacher may need to participate.

○ Students ask each other the questions for around two minutes.

○ Signal the change of partner.

Work it Out with Phrasal Verbs Extra practice

9 Extra practice 9: Shopping

20–25 mins

- Split students in to two groups: customers and shop owners. Give them the appropriate worksheet.

- Students make notes on what they might say and how to include the phrasal verbs in a positive or negative dialogue. Provide examples if necessary (e.g. *I have to pick up some t-shirts for my holiday tomorrow!*; *Don't accuse me of ripping you off!*; *You'd better snap it up before it sells out!*; etc.).

- Put students in pairs (a customer and a shop owner) to have their conversation.

- Students change partners for further practice.

10 Extra practice 10: Health

15–20 mins

- Give a set of cards to each student. For large classes you can issue fewer cards.

- Students walk around the classroom and choose a card from their set.

- Depending on the instructions on the card, students ask their partners to act out, write, or describe the phrasal verb.

Work it Out with Phrasal Verbs

Extra practice 1

Verb	Particle	Synonym	Definition
ASK	AROUND	TO INQUIRE	to speak to many people to find the answer
CALM	DOWN	TO RELAX	to become, or make somebody become, less excited, anxious or upset
CHECK	OUT	TO EXAMINE	to take a look at something
CHEER	UP	TO COMFORT	to make yourself, or someone else, feel happier
KEEP	ON	TO CONTINUE	to maintain doing something
LOOK	INTO	TO ANALYSE	to do research to find something
SET	ON	TO BE DETERMINED	to be sure you are going to achieve the objective you have in mind
SPEAK	UP	TO EXPRESS OWN IDEA	to express opinions freely and honestly
TAKE	ON	TO ACCEPT	to begin, or take responsibility for, something
THINK	OVER	TO CONSIDER	to reflect on something

Work it Out with Phrasal Verbs

Extra practice 2

A   My parents split up when I was young, and my father moved to the city.

B   When my mum is at work, my grandmother looks after me and my siblings.

C   My brother is really naughty, my mum tells him off all the time!

D   This is me, Lara. I grew up in a very large family and I'm the youngest.

E   I was brought up on a farm, where I learnt to feed the chickens and milk the cows.

F   My grandmother is my hero. She's worked hard all her life and she's very patient with her grandchildren. That's why I look up to her.

G   I could never fall out with my sister – she's my best friend. We spend so much time together.

H   People always say I look like my mum, I just hope my personality is like hers, too! She always makes me feel better when I'm going through a difficult time.

I   I don't get on with my brother. We fight all the time.

Work it Out with Phrasal Verbs

Extra practice 3

Set A

Colleague 1
You've just been on a wonderful holiday. You're telling your friend all about it, but your colleague wants to know all the details. Answer your friend's questions.

Remember to use as many phrasal verbs from this lesson as possible!

Colleague 2
Your colleague has just come back from a lovely holiday. Ask as many questions as you can about their holiday.

Remember to use as many phrasal verbs from this lesson as possible!

Set B

Holiday maker
You've just come back from a very expensive holiday, but unfortunately many things went wrong. You're describing the issues you had to your travel agent and you're hoping to receive some compensation.

Remember to use as many phrasal verbs from this lesson as possible!

Travel agent
One of your clients has just come back from a very expensive holiday you organised for them. Unfortunately there were many problems and your client is now complaining. They would like some compensation.

Remember to use as many phrasal verbs from this lesson as possible!

Set C

Friend 1
You and your friend are planning a holiday together. Decide all the details about your holiday. You might need to compromise to find an agreement.

Remember to use as many phrasal verbs from this lesson as possible!

Friend 2
You and your friend are planning a holiday together. Decide all the details about your holiday. You might need to compromise to find an agreement.

Remember to use as many phrasal verbs from this lesson as possible!

Set D

Hotel receptionist
You're working as a hotel receptionist. A customer approaches you with many questions. You try to be helpful at the beginning of the conversation, but then you lose your patience and you want the customer to leave.

Remember to use as many phrasal verbs from this lesson as possible!

Hotel guest
You've just arrived at the hotel you're staying at. You've never been there before. Ask lots of questions about hotel rules, activities and restaurants in the area.

Remember to use as many phrasal verbs from this lesson as possible!

Work it Out with Phrasal Verbs

Extra practice 4

Student A	Student B
Ask out *Invite, person, boy, girl, dinner*	**Break up** *Finish, end, sad, argue, fight*
Stand up *Meet, avoid, date, forget, message*	**Settle down** *Start, children, family, life, house*
Lead (someone) on *Interested, finish, end, think, keen*	**Get on with (someone)** *Friends, friendly, like, connection, relationship*
Make up *Friends, argument, unhappy, again, talk*	**Hit it off** *Connection, straight away, like, attracted, good*
Fall for (someone) *Love, begin, start, like, attracted*	**Turn down** *Invite, invitation, no, refuse, go out*

Work it Out with Phrasal Verbs

Extra practice 5

1. You shouldn't eat *wolfed down / gone off* food.

2. I'd find it easy to *cut out / top up* sugary food from my diet.

3. I prefer to *put on / eat out* than *serve up / eat in*.

4. I often *pick at / fill up* food between meals.

5. I never *wolf down / serve up* my food. I always take my time to enjoy the meal.

6. If I don't finish all my food in a restaurant, I'll often *top up / take away* the leftovers.

7. You should *wash down / top up* ladies' glasses first.

8. I like to *slice up / wash down* my lunch with a fizzy drink.

9. *Slicing up / cutting out* a cake at a wedding is a tradition in my country.

10. If you eat a balanced diet, you're less likely to *take away / put on* weight.

11. Sometimes, I *fill myself up / eat out* with snacks – then I'm not hungry for a meal.

12. I often make a mess when I'm *filling up / serving up* a cooked meal.

Work it Out with Phrasal Verbs

Extra practice 6

1 To share updates on each other's lives.

2 To pass an object to someone.

3 To do exercise.

4 To understand something or to solve a problem.

5 A short visit.

6 To remove something that is tight or attached to something else.

7 To spend the night at somebody else's house.

8 To join a course or an activity.

9 To read something in detail.

10 To prepare something quickly.

A	Pop _____.	F	Sign _____ _____ (something).
B	Hand _____ (something).	G	Sleep _____.
C	Rustle (something) _____.	H	Work _____.
D	Go _____ (something).	I	Figure _____.
E	Catch _____.	J	Peel (something) _____.

Work it Out with Phrasal Verbs

Extra practice 7A

Thief Finally Caught

By Lucia Castro

Last night, Jeremy Severn, from Edinburgh, Scotland, was finally **(1)**_____ for stealing thousands of pounds worth of gold jewelry from several houses he **(2)**_____ last month. He was finally captured after he thought he had **(3)**_____ the crime, but was **(4)**_____ by traffic police due to his back light being broken. He was stopped with his getaway driver, Amelia. Luckily, the police recognised both suspects and arrested them. Jeremy is now serving six years in prison for his crime. His driver, Amelia, was **(5)**_____.

Work it Out with Phrasal Verbs

Extra practice 7B

A Timely Crime

By Fawaz Shah

Events unfolded in San Francisco, California, last Saturday as two crimes were carried out simultaneously across the city.

A loud explosion was heard around 9 p.m. by residents who described the noise as 'deafening'. The sound came from an abandoned factory, which had been **(1)**_____ in the east of the city. Police rushed to the scene to find the suspect had disappeared. However, CCTV shows JJ Boyd – a 23-year-old from the local area – leaving explosives by the back entrance. Police believe JJ was creating a distraction while another crime was happening across the city. Charlie Boyd, 22, **(2)**_____ the jail cell the police had been holding him in. He **(3)**_____ two police officers as he rushed out of the door. He had originally been arrested for selling fake designer handbags in the local market. He was expected to receive a sentence of four years in prison.

Police are now **(4)**_____ the house they believe the two suspects are hiding in. They are urging the suspects to **(5)**_____ and face only ten years. If not, they may both face up to 25 years in prison.

1

2

3

4

5

Work it Out with Phrasal Verbs

Extra practice 8

Set A

1. Have you ever taken over anybody's role, at work or at school?

2. What contract have you renewed that has recently run out?

3. Do you know anyone who has got ahead in their career?

4. What do you think the procedure is to take someone on?

5. When you come up with a plan or an idea, do you run it by anyone for advice? Who?

6. Have you ever signed up for a course to learn a new skill? What was it?

7. During a lesson or a meeting, do you ever note down what has been said?

8. Have you ever called off an important meeting? Why? Who with?

Set B

1. Have you ever gone ahead with a plan despite other people's recommendations? Why?

2. Have you ever sold off anything you own?

3. Have you ever stayed behind at school or at work to finish a project? Why?

4. Have you ever cut down on anything in order to save money? What was it?

5. Have you ever been ripped off? Where? What did you buy?

6. What negative effects might there be when you are snowed under with work?

7. How can a company deal with employees who often call in sick?

8. Do you enjoy carrying out tasks under pressure? Why/Why not?

Work it Out with Phrasal Verbs

Extra practice 9A

You are a customer.

Choose an item you want to buy:

Explain why you need this item (use one or more phrasal verbs below):

Pick (something) up	Stock up (on something)	Shop around (for something)

Give more details about the item you would like:

Colour	Brand	Style

Ask for the price.

Comment on the price (use one or more phrasal verbs below):

Knock (something) off	Fork out	Rip (somebody) off

Work it Out with Phrasal Verbs

Extra practice 9B

You are the owner of a shop.

A customer would like to buy one of these items:

The customer tells you why they need the item.

Respond, using one or more phrasal verbs below:

Pick (something) up	Stock up (on something)	Shop around (for something)

The customer gives you more details about the item they would like.

Make some comments, using one or more phrasal verbs below:

Snap (something) up	Sell out	Skimp on (something)

When asked, tell the customer the price of the item.

Respond to your customer's comments, using one or more phrasal verbs below:

Knock (something) off	Cough up	Rip (somebody) off

Work it Out with Phrasal Verbs

Extra practice 10

Act out: **A blocked-up nose**	Write a sentence with: **Break out**

Give advice on how to: **Build up your strength**	Talk about: **Coming down with the flu**

Give advice on how to: **Fight off a cold**	Give a definition of: **Get over (an illness)**

Describe a tradition in your country for when someone: **Passes away**	Act out: **Pass out**

Write a sentence with: **Pick a (non-serious illness) up**	Act out: **Throw up**

Phrasal verb reference

Work it Out with Phrasal Verbs   Phrasal verb reference

Work out 1. Advice

Ask around – to speak to many people to find the answer

Calm down – to become, or make somebody become, less excited, anxious or upset

Check out – to take a look at something

Cheer up – to make yourself, or someone else, feel happier

Keep on – to maintain doing something

Look into (something) – to do research to find something

Set on (doing something) – to be sure you are going to achieve a planned objective

Speak up – to express opinions freely and honestly

Take on – to begin, or take responsibility for, something

Think over – to reflect on something

Work out 2. Family

Bring up – to take care of someone until they are an adult

Fall out (with) – to argue with someone and to no longer have a relationship

Get on/along (with) – to have a good relationship with someone

Grow up – the process by which you went from being a child, to an adult

Look after – to take care of someone/something

Look like – to look similar to another person

Look up to – to admire someone

Split up – to end a relationship (e.g. a couple separating, often divorcing)

Tell off – to reprimand/scold someone

Work out 3. Holidays

Check in – to confirm that you have arrived at a hotel or airport

Check out – to leave a hotel after returning your room key

Eat out – to have a meal in a restaurant, not at home

Get in/into – to enter a place

Go away – to leave a place (often to spend time somewhere else, usually on holiday)

Take (some time) off – to have a break from work for a few days

Take off – to begin to fly (e.g. an aeroplane or helicopter)

Wait around – to wait somewhere for something

Work out 4. Relationships

Ask out – to invite someone to go out with you

Break up/split up – to end a relationship

Fall for – to begin to love someone

Get on with – to have a good relationship with someone

Hit it off – to have an instant connection with someone

Lead on – to make someone think you are interested in them, even though you are not

Make up – to become friends after having an argument

Settle down – to start a family and have children

Stand up – if someone arranges to meet you and they don't come

Turn down – to say 'no' to an invitation to go out

Work out 5. Eating and drinking

Cut out – to eliminate something from your diet

Eat in – to have a meal at home (not in a restaurant)

Eat out – to have a meal at a restaurant (not at home)

Fill yourself up – to eat so much that you are no longer hungry

Go off – when the food has passed its expiry date and can no longer be eaten

Pick at – to have many small snacks instead of a full meal

Put on (weight) – becoming bigger and heavier

Serve up – to put food onto plates, ready to be eaten

Slice up – to cut food into pieces to be shared (e.g. a pizza)

Take away – to order food from a restaurant but to eat it at home

Top up (the glass) – to add more drink when there isn't much left

Wash down (with) – to have a drink during a meal

Wolf down – to eat very quickly and in a large quantity

Work out 6. Dreams

Catch up – to share updates on each other's lives

Figure out – to understand something or to solve a problem

Go over (something) – to read something in detail

Hand over (something) – to pass an object to someone

Peel (something) off – to remove something that is tight or attached to something else

Pop over – to visit someone for a short period of time

Sign up for – to join a course or an activity

Sleep over – to spend the night at somebody else's house

Work out – to do exercise

Work out 7. Crime

Blow up – to create an explosion

Break in – to enter a building that is not yours

Get away with – to avoid punishment for a crime you have committed

Knock (someone) out – to fight with someone until they lose consciousness

Let (someone) off – to not punish someone for their crime or bad actions

Lock up – when someone is put in prison

Pull (someone) over – when the police signal for your car to move to the side of the road

Stake out – to sit outside a place to observe what is happening

Turn (someone) in – to tell the authorities of someone who has committed a crime

Work out 8. Business

Snowed under – to have a lot of work to do

Call in (sick) – to inform your workplace that you are too sick to work

Call off – to stop something from happening, such as a wedding or a meeting

Carry out – to perform or complete a task

Come up with – to think of something, such as an idea or a plan

Cut down – to decrease the quantity of something used

Get ahead – to be successful in one's job

Go ahead with – to start doing something after waiting for someone's permission

Note down – to write something down to avoid forgetting it

Rip off – to cheat someone by charging them too much money for something

Run by – to share your ideas with someone to hear their opinion

Run out – when something comes to an end, such as a contract or an agreement

Sell off – to sell something at a lower price because you need the money

Sign up – to subscribe or to join a group or a course

Stay behind – to not leave a place (school/work) when other people leave

Take on – to employ someone

Take over – to replace someone in their role

Work out 9. Shopping

Cough up – to pay someone, usually when you don't want to

Fork out (for something) – to pay more for something than you expected to pay

Knock (something) off – to reduce the price of something by a stated amount

Pick (something) up – to buy something spontaneously

Rip (somebody) off – to make someone pay more than they should

Sell out – to sell all of something; to run out of stock

Shop around (for something) – to compare the price of the same item in different shops

Skimp on (something) – to use too little of something in order to make it last longer

Snap (something) up – to buy something quickly, usually before the stock runs out

Stock up (on something) – to buy a large quantity of something

Work out 10. Health

Block up – to stop something moving through something else

Break out – when you develop a sudden skin irritation

Build up (your strength) – to slowly become stronger after an illness

Come down with (an illness) – to become ill with an illness that is not very serious

Fight off – to attempt to free yourself from an illness

Get over – to recover from an illness

Pass away – to die

Pass out – to lose consciousness; to faint

Pick (something) up – to catch a non-serious illness from another person or place

Throw up – to vomit

Download the digital components

Downloadable content:

- Front-of-class presentations
- Worksheets
- Extra practice activities
- Phrasal verb overview handout
- Phrasal verb reference

Download url:

- www.prosperityeducation.net/phrasal

Instructions:

- Go to url
- Password: TIAB
- Select the *Work it Out with Phrasal Verbs* book image
- Select content to download

Acknowledgements

Artworks composited from Noun Project icons: Group by Oksana Latysheva; Grandmother and granddaughter, Woman Holding, Mother Leaving, Hands, Snatch, Fighting, Sad Child, Police, Break In, Thief, Man Dreaming, Pajamas, Sleep, and Uppercut by Gan Khoon Lay; Arrow by IconTrack; Farm house by ProSymbols; Family by mungang kim; Boy by Adrien Coquet; Girl by Hawraa Alsalman; Girl and Girl by Adrien Coquet; Going to school by ProSymbols; Energy by Caitlin George; Jail by Adrien Coquet; Police by Sergey Demushkin; Jump by Brad Avison; Open jail door with three bars by Richard Slade; Demolition by Luis Prado; Prison Break by Chameleon Design; Binoculars by Luis Prado; Man by Brad Avison; Couch by Vectors Point; Laptop by Gilad Sotil; Polo shirt by Laymik; Timer by Rohith MS; presentation by Maxim Kulikov; Tick and cross: Pass or Fail by Ray Design; Presentation by Adrien Coquet; Uptight by auttapol; Laugh by Aneeque Ahmed.

www.ingramcontent.com/pod-product-compliance
Lightning Source LLC
Chambersburg PA
CBHW081919090526
44591CB00014B/2398